The F Every Leader Should Do

Leadership Lessons
for a Changing Church

by

JESSE L. WILSON

Watersprings

The First Thing Every Leader Should Do
Published by
Watersprings Media House, LLC.
P.O. Box 1284
Olive Branch, MS 38654
www.waterspringsmedia.com
Contact publisher for bulk orders and permission requests.

Copyright © 2017 by Jesse L. Wilson

All rights reserved. No part of this publication may be reproduced, distributed, or transmitted in any form or by any means, including photocopying, recording, or other electronic or mechanical methods, without the prior written permission of the publisher, except in the case of brief quotations embodied in critical reviews and certain other noncommercial uses permitted by copyright law.
Printed in the United States of America.

Scripture quotations taken from the Holy Bible, New International Version®. NIV® Copyright 1973, 1978, 1984 by International Bible Society. Used by permission of Zondervan. All rights reserved.

Scripture quotations marked "ESV" are taken from *The Holy Bible, English Standard Version.* Copyright © 2000; 2001 by Crossway Bibles, a division of Good News Publishers. Used by permission. All rights reserved.

Library of Congress Control Number: 2017958975

ISBN-10: 0-9988249-4-1
ISBN-13: 978-0-9988249-4-9

TABLE OF CONTENTS

LEADERSHIP DEVELOPMENT 5
Three Words Every Leader Hates 6
Christ to Critics: "Stop Attacking My Wife!" 10
The Investment Every Leader Must Make 15
Jamal Bryant, Jimmy Swaggart, and You- 18
Cursing Christians: Can Good People Say Bad Words? 24
How Long Should it Hurt-Challenging a Myth About Grieving 28
Grace! Three Things My Wedding Taught Me 30
The First Thing Every Leader Should Do 34

CHURCH GROWTH & DEVELOPMENT 37
Three Common Sense Keys to Church Growth 38
What To Do When Your Church Is Dying? 44
When Should We Close a Local Church? 48
Chick-fil-A: What Your Church Could Learn 51
A Martian, a Meeting, and the Mission 59
How Adventist Evangelism, Hurts Adventist Evangelism 62

WORSHIP 67
Seven Reasons Churches Don't Sing 68
Three More Reasons Churches Don't Sing 72
Everything That Shouts Ain't Pentecostal 76

ADVENTIST ISSUES 80
Three Reasons Adventists Should Celebrate Easter 81
Trick or Treat! Should Christians Celebrate Halloween? 85
Camp Meetings: Here to Stay or Time to Go? 90
PELC Preachers, Stay Off the Stage 94
Why Freddy Haynes is Speaking at PELC 98
What Do They See When We Say Adventist? 101

CULTURE & SOCIAL JUSTICE 103
Three Reasons I Pray for Trump 104
What the Church Lost When Trump Won 108

TABLE OF CONTENTS

When Some Trump Criticism is just...Dumb 113
How to Keep HBCU Presidents at Home 117
Three Words That Could Cripple The Race Crisis 121
Why Adventist Ministers March 126
The Sharpton I Know 130
Michael Nixon, Andrews U, and Race 134

LEADERSHIP ICONS 139

Ministers Who Marked My Ministry- 140
  Bishop Gilbert Patterson 140
  Pastor Robert Leslie Willis 144
  Dr. E. E. Cleveland 148

The Second Thing That Every Leader Should Do 152

LEADERSHIP DEVELOPMENT

1

THREE WORDS EVERY LEADER HATES

There are three words every successful leader is destined to hear. They represent the nameless, faceless opposition that can distract, depress or demoralize you if you're not careful. And those three words are:

"People are saying."

These words follow successful leaders because they are generally the result of movement and change. They are like a sniper's bullet. Difficult to trace, but impossible to ignore.

To be clear, not all change is good change. I refer you to an earlier chapter which identified, "The First Thing Every Leader Should Do." The answer is nothing. Do nothing but listen and learn. But after you've listened and learned it's time to move. And when you move there will always be those who are reluctant to move with you or the program.

Unfortunately, few detractors these days seem interested in attaching their names to criticism, especially in the church. So, they find ways to make their concerns known to a third party. The infamous "unnamed source."

One day, I was channel surfing and landed on a lively argument on CNN. They were discussing Trump's recent trip to the Middle East and Europe. A couple of the panelists were arguing that Trump came back depressed, lonely, and angry. They argued with such detail that I was sure that someone had overheard

Melania or Ivanka. But then I read the title of the segment, "Unnamed sources: Trump returns lonely, frustrated and angry."

As much as I dislike the actions of Trump, for me, unnamed sources are no better. Unnamed, unidentified, unethical criticism and rumor are undermining relationships from the statehouse to the church house.

I was discussing the damage of unnamed sources on my Facebook page and someone sent me an interesting link. It was to the National Public Radio Ethics Handbook. As I skimmed through some of their policies concerning anonymous sourcing, fairness, and ethics in communication, it struck me that the church could learn from some of their guidelines. Let's see how they suggest you should handle critics who would prefer to go unnamed.

If you don't have a name, you don't have a story.

That's generally the approach you should take when people approach you with information they don't want to attach a name to. Now, some situations are too volatile or even too dangerous to reveal names. Whistleblowers perform a valuable function in certain environments. But as a rule, criticism should be addressed directly. If a source is not willing to go on the record there is possibly something flawed about the information, the motivation, the timing, or the source.

Determine if the source is reliable and knowledgeable.

Some people are just messy. Their history confirms that they are neither reliable nor knowledgeable. You can pretty much predict that where there's trouble, they will be involved. Criticism and gossip are practically a sport to them.

They gravitate toward controversy like a moth to a flame. Don't allow yourself to be inadvertently triangled into their "sport."

Press the source hard.

This counsel from the ethics manual was interesting. In essence, it encourages you to stop the foolishness before it starts. Encourage the critic to drop the matter if that is possible. If they refuse, press them to voice their criticism directly and privately. Sounds like Matthew 18 to me.

Remember online sources should be on the record too.

Marriages, reputations, and careers are being destroyed in seconds by online assassins. And even if the attackers regret their words, the words remain for all to see, for generations to come.

Now that was some counsel from the National Public Radio ethics guide on ethics in communication. But I have a better source, a higher authority. The Bible provides a wealth of counsel on how to criticize correctly.

> *"If anyone thinks he is religious and does not bridle his tongue but deceives his heart, this person's religion is worthless." (James 1:26)*

> *"Do not speak evil against one another, brothers." (James 4:11)*

> *"Let all bitterness and wrath and anger and clamor and slander be put away from you, along with all malice. Be kind to one another, tenderhearted, forgiving one another, as God in Christ forgave you." (Eph. 4:31-32)*

Let me add my two cents.

- Study Matthew 18.
- Know the difference between constructive and destructive criticism.
- Make sure you pick the right time and place.
- Make sure that you are the right person.
- Be specific.
- Focus on the behavior and not the person.
- Know when to stop.

Oh yeah, this stuff is a lot easier said than done. But it's well worth the effort.

2

CHRIST TO CRITICS: "STOP ATTACKING MY WIFE!"

Here's the thing. Some people are going to read the title of this blog and totally miss the message of this blog. What do I mean? This is what I mean. It is absolutely appropriate to criticize the church. Frankly, we probably don't criticize the church enough. We are counseled in Ephesians 4:17 to speak the truth in love and that passage is in the context of the church.

But we must not only speak the truth in love, we must speak truth to power. Walter Brueggemann, one of the most prolific theologians in the modern era, reminds us in his book, *Truth Speaks to Power*, that Jesus was a persistent thorn in the flesh of unethical power brokers inside and outside the church. Church criticism is critical for church development.

But there is a difference between criticism and attack. Frankly, they feel about the same. For most of us the difference between constructive and destructive criticism is pretty clear. Constructive criticism is the criticism you give. Destructive criticism is the criticism you get!

But attacks are more personal and generally counterproductive. They rarely offer a solution and they are often too cowardly for face to face confrontation. Attacks are rarely looking for real answers. In fact, when you offer answers they find more questions. Attacks come from the left and right, from conservatives and liberals.

I don't have any steps or keys or laws or secrets for addressing church attacks but let me offer some observations for those who are prone to attack.

OBSERVATION #1: Examine Your Own Motives

Church attacks often say as much about the attacker as they do the church. Why do you return to this spot over and over? Why is the topic so sensitive to you? Make sure that the church has not become a convenient platform for you to project your own issues. Mad people are often hurt people, and hurt people hurt people. I'm not dismissing valid criticism, but attacks are often coming from a damaged place.

OBSERVATION #2: The Good Old Days Weren't All That Good

People who are constantly calling for that "old time religion", have selective amnesia. The church has always had problems- big problems. And I'm not just referring to your local church or the contemporary church. Just look at the "glory days" of the precious New Testament church.

The Church at Corinth had so many divisive issues that Paul addressed them in two long letters. Members were sleeping around. The worship service was out of control and members were regularly suing each other.

The Church at Galatia battled over the nature of the law, the role of the law, and freedom of conscience.

The Church at Ephesus struggled with the nature of the church, the function of church leaders, they had problems with domestic relations, and the nature of spiritual warfare.

The Churches at Colossae and Thessalonica struggled with the nature of Christ-which incidentally was an early issue in the Adventist Church. There was confusion about the second Advent and some of the members had retreated to a mountain to wait for Jesus to come!

The Church at Phillipi had fights at "business meetings" that were so intense that Paul called out the trouble makers by name.

So, if you're looking for a return to the good old days-don't.

OBSERVATION #3: Make Sure You Have the Whole Story

I can't tell you the number of times my perspective has changed after I've heard the whole story. I look at the number of posts online of Christians complaining about how they've been mistreated by the church. I'm sure that a large number of them, if not most of them, are true. But I remember the members I've pastored over the years who practically lived off the special assistance of the church but complained to outsiders that the church "never helps members in need." Really? Get the whole story.

OBSERVATION #4: Church Attacks Damage You and Yours

Now this one is fairly obvious. The church is not brick and mortar, the church is you and me. When you unfairly attack the church, you attack yourself. You could be undermining the very hospital you'll need for your own recovery. And it gets worse. The next generation is watching and listening.

As I said earlier, the church needs more thoughtful criticism. We are paying a steep price for being painfully political or downright unchristian. Some of our conference constituency meetings and decisions by our conference committees have had university classrooms buzzing. But the way we address these church problems can either raise a generation of constructive critics or hopeless cynics.

OBSERVATION #5: If You Can Identify a Problem, You Can Probably Identify a Solution

Here is where you see the value of criticism versus the damage of attack. Every great church reformation has begun with criticism. The prophets leveled blistering criticism at Israel. Jesus was not a bit bashful about bashing the religious right. But it was all done with an eye toward reformation. It was done with a clear solution in mind.

And here's another critical distinction between attack and criticism. Attack generally functions from outside in. Criticism generally functions from inside out. In other words, you are generally in the best position to make lasting change if you're operating from the inside. If you are a part of the group. Not always, but more often than not.

I hear it all the time in one form or another.

> *"I'm spiritual but I'm not religious."*
> *"People love Jesus, but they don't like the church."*

Think about it. That's like you saying to me, "I love you man, but I frankly can't stand your wife!" My wife and I have been married for more than 33 years. That statement is not going to go over very well with me.

The Bible makes it clear that Christ loves the church. That Christ is married to the church. For better or worse. For richer or poorer. In sickness and in health. Even through death. Be careful how you treat His wife.

3

THE INVESTMENT EVERY LEADER MUST MAKE

This quotation is over 150 years old and still as powerful and relevant as the day Ellen White wrote it, "Our first duty before God and our fellow beings is that of self-development." *(Signs of the Times Nov. 17, 1890)*

Self-development. Some see it as synonymous with selfishness, but that is a tragic mistake. When you are at your best it not only benefits you but everyone you serve. Stunted growth is a problem personally and professionally.

The ministry seems to have more than its share of arrested development. I'm sure that this problem is not limited to full time ministry, but far too many religious leaders undervalue the need for continued growth and development. Let me list 5 "selfish" areas that religious leaders would do well to strengthen.

The Leader's Faith

The leader's ministry is no stronger than the leader's devotional life. And that's a challenge because the work is never done, especially if you are a pastor. Weddings, funerals, business and board meetings, counseling, church conflicts, and the list goes on. If the pastor isn't careful she can find herself developing sermons without developing herself. I know that gender reference upset some of you. Get over it.

The Leader's Family

This is self-development 101. If there is trouble at home, it won't be long before there's trouble at work. It would be helpful for religious leaders to remember the value of professional care and counseling. Not just for the member but for you. The best thing that many religious leaders could do is to seek out a caring and competent counselor. And I'm not talking about the Mighty Counselor either. I'm talking about one that will charge you by the hour!

The Leader's Health

I'm not going to beat a dead horse. *(Dead horse. Unintentionally appropriate...and funny in a morbid kinda way. But I digress.)* Get some exercise. Get some rest. Take a vacation. The work will never end, but you will if you don't wake up.

The Leader's Finances

The way my church compensates retired leaders is a sin. The only thing worse is the way their spouses are treated financially. You can commit to 30 years or more of full time ministry and not expect to receive $2000 per month at retirement-if that much!

I'll never forget spending an afternoon with one of the greatest evangelists the Adventist Church ever produced. He had baptized thousands, written extensively, lectured endlessly, and loved the church deeply. But now in retirement, we spoke in his kitchen which doubled as his library. The entire apartment was clean but cramped. He seemed a bit embarrassed by it all. Tears literally filled my eyes as I left this man who had meant so much to my ministry and my church.

I don't doubt that personal decisions influenced his situation, but so what? It was his devotion to the church and the demands of the church that influenced most of those decisions. I get upset when I think about it. Underpaid for life, and disrespected at death. The church should do better but religious leaders don't have the luxury to wait. Take care of your finances.

The Leader's Professional Growth

For most religious leaders, their professional growth ends when they leave the seminary. That's unfortunate. Frankly, you don't even know the right questions to ask until you become active in ministry. Much of front-loaded education is not wasted but misplaced. Continuing education is critical.

Self-development and continuing education can be costly, especially on a tight budget. But the cost of ignorance and lack of preparation is much steeper. So, let's step it up. Faith, family, health, finances, professional growth: They are investments that pay eternal dividends.

4

JAMAL BRYANT, JIMMY SWAGGART, AND YOU—CAN A FALLEN LEADER BE RESTORED?

This week I made my annual pilgrimage to the Hampton Ministers Conference. Listening to Lance Watson, Rudolph McKissick, Marcus Cosby was amazing. Seeing them and former Hampton President William Houston Curtis reminded me of the lasting relationships we've established with these preachers through our own minister's conference, PELC. It was also good to hear Claybon Lea and see Freddie Haynes who will both be with us in December.

As soon as I sat down in the morning service to hear Cosby, my mind went to the morning service a year earlier. The preacher was Jamal Bryant, pastor of the 12,000-member Empowerment Temple in Baltimore. It wasn't unusual to see a packed house that early in the morning because he's an amazing preacher and gifted communicator.

But there was a strange buzz in the air that morning. Just a few days earlier the internet exploded with details and pictures of a young lady claiming an affair and child with Bryant. Many wondered if Hampton would withdraw their speaking invitation. But not only did he speak, his father Bishop John Bryant introduced him, his gifted mother sat behind him, and he proceeded to preach a classic message to a receptive crowd.

Later I saw him interviewed by Roland Martin as he admitted to infidelities that ended his marriage, confused his children, and battered his reputation. The internet exploded, and his church was devastated.

Go with me to Chicago. Pastor Charles Jenkins and the Fellowship M.B. Church dominated the gospel music charts in 2012. I worshipped with them this year on Pentecost Sunday. Their hit single "My God is Awesome" was recognized by BMI as the most played single on gospel radio that year. Handpicked by the legendary Clay Evans to replace him as pastor of Fellowship, Jenkins was taking an already popular church to a whole new level.

Then it happened. Rumors had been swirling, and on Easter Sunday 2014, he admitted to an affair with a church employee. The internet exploded, and his church was devastated.

Let's go to Atlanta. One weekday several years ago, we walked through the empty sanctuary of the New Birth Baptist Church in Lithonia. Our church, Madison Mission, was planning to build and we wanted to observe other churches and talk to them about their buildings.

But it wasn't long before the conversation shifted from the building to the pastor, Bishop Eddie Long. He had been accused of having inappropriate relationships with several young men. There were even pictures circulating. The internet exploded, and the church was devastated.

Finally, let's head to New Orleans. Jimmy Swaggart was the most popular evangelical evangelist next to Billy Graham in the 70s and 80s. From the city of Baton Rouge, Louisiana, he led the Family Worship Center and the international Jimmy Swaggart Ministries. But it was in New Orleans that he was caught with prostitutes in 1988 and three years later in 1991. The budding internet exploded, and his church and ministry were devastated.

Four unfortunate situations. Very different in some ways but absolutely the same in one significant way. Each of these men remained as pastor of his church. They all paused a while and returned to their pulpits – some within weeks.

This problem of fallen leaders is not new. It's difficult to determine if the incidents are growing that rapidly or if the internet has just made us more aware of the problem. One thing is for sure. The results are clearly wrecking families and undermining the credibility of religious leaders, especially in the minds of young people.

I cringe when I go online and read the comments and hear the critics after a religious leader publicly falls. I can deal with the silly attacks from outsiders, but I'm really impacted by the deep hurt and disillusionment of insiders. I'll never forget the pained look on a woman's face who questioned aloud how Charles Jenkins could have penned and performed her favorite song, "My God is Awesome" while carrying on an affair. Tough one.

Can pastors be restored? Of course, they can! The aim of the gospel is restoration, and no one is exempt- including pastors. Of course, pastors and religious leaders can be restored. But that's probably not the best question. A better question is probably, should they be? And how about:

- Does restoration mean returning to the same pulpit?
- How long should a pastor remain out of the pulpit?
- Is sexual sin in a different category?
- Does the "above reproach" mandate for pastors mean a lifetime of perfect service?

- What about church discipline and religious leaders?
- What about the damage to the church family?
- What about the damage to the pastor's family?

Now, I've noticed that where you stand on this issue is often influenced by where you sit. If the issue of fallen leaders is basically theory to you, then you probably lean heavily toward grace. If you have had first-hand experience with the issue, you probably still lean toward grace, but with a healthy dose of corrective discipline. Incidentally, the two are not mutually exclusive.

This issue is difficult because no two situations are exactly alike. The clear majority of Christian denominations and Christians themselves favor restoring fallen Christian leaders for most offensives. By that, I mean returning them to church fellowship, membership and even ministry. There is far less support for a minister or leader returning to the exact location of the offense – the scene of the "crime."

This topic defies neat and tidy answers, but let me share a few observations.

Every leader has been restored.

There are no unfallen leaders. Some fall privately, others fall publicly, but they all fall. The goal of the gospel is restoration. No one is exempt, including local pastors. The best and the brightest have fallen. God's honor roll is replete with liars, cheaters, robbers, philanderers, and even murderers. Do the math: Abraham, Moses, Samson, Solomon, David. Great men, but I'm not sure I'd leave my wife with some of them!

But the Bible is big on restoration. It's interesting that the basic definition of restoration is to return a thing to its former condition. But the biblical definition often goes much further. The restored condition is often better than the original. Amazing!

 There is no restoration without heartfelt repentance.

"Repentance includes sorrow for sin and a turning away from it. We will not renounce sin unless we see its sinfulness; until we turn away from it in heart, there will be no real change in the life" (Steps to Christ p. 24).

Real repentance produces real fruit. Not immediately and certainly not without effort, but repentance produces fruit. Sincere sorry is a fruit of real repentance. Restitution is a fruit of real repentance. Clear confession is fruit of real repentance. Real repentance not only changes actions but attitudes.

I mentioned last week that I listened to Jamal Bryant preach just days after his affair was uncovered. I was willing to give him the benefit of the doubt until he took a not-so-subtle swipe at his accuser in his message. He lost me. His actions didn't illustrate a genuine sorrow for what he'd done. In that statement and in interviews to follow, he seemed combative and defensive.

It also illustrated the imbalance of power that is so often a part of sexual sin and harassment. It seemed that he used the Hampton Minister's Conference platform to go after an accuser who was totally incapable of defending herself or even responding.

Restoration and reassignment are not the same.

Restoration is a return to your original condition in Christ, not necessarily your original position in the church. The grace and forgiveness that God offers freely is never without cost or consequence. There are situations where it is clearly unwise and even dangerous to return a Christian leader to a position of authority. An embezzler can and should be restored to church fellowship, but it's probably not wise for her to return as church treasurer. A pedophile should not be returned to children's ministry. A philanderer shouldn't lead the singles.

The shifting of bad leaders from one location to another has seriously undermined confidence in the Catholic priesthood in particular and the ministry in general. I personally support moving a fully recovered, restored, and repentant leader to another location to resume leadership in ministry. But it demonstrates that even a move that's good for a restored pastor, might still be bad for a church struggling to regain public trust.

A blog seems so insufficient for a topic like this. I have about six pages of notes staring at me on my desk, but I'm stopping here. I pray for the countless thousands who have been hurt by corruption that the church has ignored. I pray for pastors and leaders who have fallen, but by God's grace have risen to serve again. I pray for the church.

5

CURSING CHRISTIANS:
CAN GOOD PEOPLE SAY BAD WORDS?

Is it just me, or is there more cursing going on these days? Now in the spirit of full disclosure, and since my friends read this blog, I don't claim total victory in this area. But something has changed. What ever happened to the good old days of *dangs* and *darns* and the occasional *dag-nabit*? It seems like this generation has skipped that stage and gone straight to f-bombs and s-words.

Note: If the mention of f-bombs and s-words is too much for you, you might want to skip this blog. See you next week.

Timothy Jay, a Psychology professor at Massachusetts College of Liberal Arts, and the author of *Why We Curse and Cursing in America* (I couldn't make this stuff up) says that, "Our language values are shifting…Elementary teachers report that children are using more offensive language than in the past."

Well, I can't speak for elementary teachers, but I can speak for college professors. I spend most of the year on college campuses, and you can't help but notice that cursing is on the rise. You might not hear it in the library or the classroom, but you'd better brace yourself if you go to the cafeteria or gymnasium. If you listen closely, you'll wish that you hadn't listened closely!

Now let me be clear. This is not a referendum on the spirituality of this generation. My students give me faith in the future of the church. And this is not a "good old days vs. bad new days" post.

We're living in an evil age, and it's going to get worse before it gets better. But there's a problem. It's hard enough monitoring the media, I don't want to steer my little ones around clusters of Christian students.

I spoke to a classroom of university students about this cursing issue and they all agreed that it was on the rise. They cited the influence of social media, motion pictures, broadcast television and especially the lyrics of popular music. Profanity is such a pervasive part of popular culture that it seems almost impossible to escape.

But the question is, what is a Christian to do? Is it ok for Christians to curse?

Let me leave you with three brief, but bold points the Bible makes about the importance of our words.

1. Watch What You Say

"Be imitators of Christ…Nor should there be obscenity, foolish talk, or coarse joking, which are out of place, but rather thanksgiving." - Ephesians 5:1-4 NIV

"Don't let any unwholesome talk come out of your mouths…" - Ephesians 4:29 NIV

Pretty clear. It might not be a big deal to us, but it seems to make a big deal to God. And not only should we watch what our words say to others, but we should watch what our words say about ourselves.

"The mouth speaks what the heart is full of." Matthew 12:34 NLT

In other words, nothing is a clearer indicator of what's happening in your heart than what's coming out of your mouth. Scary. James says that it is impossible for us to control our tongues. But here's the good news. If we release control, He will take control of our tongues. James 3.

2. Limit What You Say

"Whoever guards his mouth preserves his life..." - Proverbs 13:3 ESV

"...Everyone should be quick to listen, slow to speak, and slow to anger." - James 1:19 NIV

This is great advice but hard advice. The plain truth is that most of us talk too much. The idea is that if we'd talk less, then we'd have fewer problems to deal with. Good luck with that. This counsel just reminds me of how impossible it is to do any of this in our own strength. But God never asks us to do what He has not empowered us to do. Give up the controls.

3. Do What You Say

"...But whoever keeps his word, in him truly the love of God is perfected." - 1 John 2:5 ESV

There it is. Watch it. Limit it. Do it. There is no greater witness to the power of God than a dependable Christian. We live in a world of missed appointments, broken promises, and casual commitments. Consistent Christians, who keep their word, are powerful witnesses.

Finally, it's clear that people, good and bad people, curse for all manner of reasons. Subjects like this tempt me to write a research paper instead of a blog. I literally could have written a small book on the issues that flow from this topic. Your comments will let me know if I need to revisit the topic. But cursing seems to be just a symptom of much larger problems that we face in this evil age.

6

How Long Should it Hurt-Challenging a Myth About Grieving

There is no person that I respect more than Dr. George Russell Seay Jr. From the same city and home church, we have known each other for years. He even had the good eyes and great fortune to marry my "best looking and sweetest sister" – he made that last comment.

He is my favorite theologian, and there is powerfully practical theology in this tribute to his late cousin, Chubby. Read it because at some point we all need it.

"The saying that time heals all wounds is misleading. First, it suggests that there is something intrinsic in time that is healing. It is not. It is time and comfort. It is the ministry of presence by those who are able to rejoice and weep with you. This sets up false expectations for the one who experienced the loss and impatience in the persons called to minister comfort.

Second, it suggests that healing will remove the sense of loss and pain in time. Those who have lost significant persons in their lives know this to be false. It is irrelevant if the person lived long or short, died suddenly or after a lengthy illness. The loss and pain remain. The intensity of pain may diminish some, but it is not eradicated.

Third, as I reflect on the significant losses in my life, I do not want the wound to heal. I am no masochist; I do not delight in pain or suffering. However, to still feel the loss says that the significance of the person and the positive memories are still with me. They still matter. In a strange way, it is the sense of loss that affirms the positive.

On this day, May 1, 42 years ago (1975) I lost my cousin Hammond Edward "Chubby" Seay. It is rare that a week goes by that something does not provoke a memory or thought of him. He was the Eldest Seay boy of the clan of Ora & Ernest Seay (my father's parents). Six years my senior, he was my hero and role model. He played the trumpet and was a member of the Raw Soul Band of Memphis, a track star in high school & college, pitcher/catcher in baseball, personable, and had a real sense of humor.

I miss him and still feel the loss. There are times that I still grieve without shame or guilt, but not without hope."

7

GRACE!
THREE THINGS MY WEDDING TAUGHT ME

My wife and I have been married 33 years this month. To say that I married up is a major understatement. *(I can almost hear, "you got that right" chorus coming from my friends. Who asked you?)* Anyway, the marriage has been easy to remember but the wedding was a blur.

But as I reflect back over that crazy day, in light of the incredible gift of grace that I've received, there are 3 lessons about that grace that I learned from my marriage.

LESSON ONE: My status changed.... Just Like That!

On the Sunday afternoon of our wedding, my wife drove to the church single and so did I.

When the music signaled the start of the service, we were both single.

When the mothers marched in, we were single.

When the wedding party assembled, we were single.

When Pastor Dew did the homily, we were sweating...but still single.

But at the moment we were pronounced man and wife, we moved from single to married-just like that!

One moment I was single, the next moment I was not. One moment I was free to do anything I wanted, the next moment I was not. One moment my ankles were free, the next moment a ball and chain…wait, I lost my train of thought. You get the point.

In a sense that's' exactly what God's grace does. It changes your status just like that! The word is justification.

"Therefore, since we have been justified through faith, we have peace with God through our Lord Jesus Christ, through whom we have gained access by faith into this grace in which we now stand." - Romans 5:1-2 NIV

Justification is an act of God's grace. It means, "to declare righteous." New Testament writers, particularly Paul, describe the word in legal terms. It is an official declaration that God has changed your status from lost to saved. It means that according to your faith in Christ, God has pardoned you, acquitted you, forgiven you, and accepted the righteousness of Christ in place of your unrighteousness. And it happened, just like that!

"Very truly I tell you, whoever hears my word and believes Him who sent me has eternal life and will not be judged but has crossed over from death to life." - John 5:24 NIV

That's good news. Just as I moved from single to married in the twinkling of an eye, God provides his salvation at the same speed. Your status changes just like that. And when God changes your status:

> You are complete in Him. *Colossians 2:10*
> You are forgiven. *Ephesians 1:7*
> You are free from condemnation. *Romans 8:1-2*
> You are a citizen of heaven. *Philippians 3:20*

You are the temple of the Holy Ghost. *1 Cor. 3:16*
You are a new creature in Jesus Christ. *2 Cor. 5:17*
You are a joint heir with Christ. *Romans 8:17*

"These things have I written unto you that believe on the name of the Son of God, that ye may know that you have eternal life..." - 1 John 5:13

We have a lifetime of Christian growth to look forward to. But by his grace we are positioned as saints right now. And it happened just like that!

LESSON NUMBER TWO: My feelings were irrelevant to my status.

I must admit. When I woke up the Monday morning following our wedding, I felt single. My feelings were the same ones I had been living with all the years prior to my wedding. Single feelings! But there was a big difference. My status had changed. I was married!

Didn't make a difference how I felt. The choice had been made. The vows had been taken. The license had been signed. The covenant had been established. My feelings were irrelevant. My status had changed. I was a married man.

And that is an important lesson of grace that many Christians struggle with constantly. "I don't feel saved, so I must be lost." It makes about as much sense as saying, "I don't feel married so I'm not." Our feelings, as valuable as they are, do not determine our standing with God. Hebrews 10:38 reminds us that the just don't live by feelings but by faith in God.

Kirk Franklin wrote a powerful blog in 2015 entitled, *"Avoiding Dark Streets with Dead Ends."* In it he thanked God for his life experiences that drove his creativity. But the sentence that stuck out to me was, "My feelings have always been an enemy of my faith." Same with many of us.

The question is simple. Whose report will you believe? God can't lie, but your feelings do. Titus 1:2. Often it takes our feelings time to catch up with the reality of our position in Christ, but I believe God.

LESSON NUMBER THREE: The wedding was free to me, but it cost an awful lot!

Actually, I didn't get the full impact of the cost of weddings until I had two girls! After each of those weddings I was reminded of how blessed I was at my own wedding…as the groom. That wedding didn't cost me a dime, but my wife's family was fully invested.

The grace that God gives, the justification that we accept, was absolutely free to us, but it came at an incredible price. So, I thank Him with my lips and my life.

"But He was wounded for our transgressions, He was bruised for our iniquities…" - Isaiah 53:5 KJV

8

THE FIRST THING EVERY LEADER SHOULD DO

L**isten.** That's the first thing that every leader should do. They should listen. Before they plan anything, they should listen. Before they announce anything, they should listen. And certainly, before they change anything, they should listen.

It seems like such a simple thing, such an obvious thing. It seems like common sense. But ask a church member, office worker, or school teacher and many of them will tell you that common sense is not as common as it used to be…at least not in this area.

Leaders, especially new leaders, need to listen before they leap. More damage is done by leaders who lead before they listen than you can imagine. What's worse is the fact that you never get a second chance to make a first impression. And if the first impression is that the leader's agenda came fully formed, trouble usually follows.

When leaders neglect the listening stage, even if there is success, often that success will never be fully shared or appreciated. It's painful to listen to successful leaders who were never really honored or appreciated by their church or organization. The problem can often be traced back to those early days. First impressions are lasting.

The Hippocratic Oath is a great example of practical wisdom. A wise physician knows that the primary responsibility to a patient is to, "First, do no harm." That's not just good wisdom for physicians, it's great counsel for pastors, presidents, principals and anyone else called to lead. As gifted as you are and as desperate as the situation may seem, in most cases, you have the luxury to take your time and listen.

Now in the spirit of full disclosure, I might not be the best source for this subject. I was always impatient in the listening stage. Especially when I confronted issues that I was confident I had the expertise to handle. But I learned. And the older I get, the more convinced I am, that a leader who misses or mishandles this listening stage, is in for a rough leadership ride.

For some young pastors, it's almost impossible to resist the urge to immediately launch that great idea or series that fascinated them in seminary. Combine that youthful zeal with a reluctance to respect any information or individual over thirty, and you have a recipe for disaster. Same for older pastors who think that what worked at one church will automatically work in another.

Why is it so important for you to look and listen early in your assignment, regardless of the organization? Because no matter how gifted you are, there are at least three things that you don't know.

1. You don't know everything!

The Barna Group's 2017 research release is entitled, *"Pastoring in the Age of Complexity."* It makes the case that there has never been a more difficult time to lead a local church than now. Why? Because of the complexity of it all. The churches they pastor defy one-size-fits-all solutions and easy answers. The world that we minister to and work in is exploding with complexity.

As it is with pastors, so it is with leaders in other vocations. It is just as complex and challenging these days to lead a marketing firm, a non-profit hospital, a charter school or even a family. Complexity challenges us all. But don't make a difficult task an impossible task, by attempting to handle it without counsel, without conversations, without listening.

2. You don't know everybody!

It's all about relationships. It's cliché but true, people still don't care how much you know until they know how much you care (I can't believe I said that. How did my mother get in the room?). You never lose when you invest time in getting to know names and faces. One of the most undervalued ministries is the ministry of presence. Just being present can make a powerful impression. It provides the soil for relationship building. It creates the capital you need now, to get things done later.

3. You don't know the culture

Churches and organizations have their own culture. Culture is the way things are done, based on shared values and history. It takes time to learn that, what is valued in one culture is vexing in another culture. What is rewarded in one culture is rejected in another culture. A leader must look and listen to understand the organizational culture. It takes time.

The leader who leaps into action before understanding the organizational culture is like the physician who prescribes medication before examining the patient. The leader who ignores organizational culture is like the parent who assumes that what worked for one child will work for the others. So, take the valuable time to look and listen early and you will reap the benefits later.

Church Growth & Development

9

THREE COMMON SENSE KEYS TO CHURCH GROWTH

The problem with common sense is that it's not quite as common as it used to be. This is particularly true in the area of church growth and evangelism. Most pastors understandably and appropriately want their churches to grow. Despite the pushback that evangelism gets these days for being a "numbers game," there is no dispute that Christ calls us to be both faithful *and* fruitful. But the pursuit of the next best thing in the church growth area can be amusing.

I walked into my home library one Sunday looking for a particular book and I almost laughed at the number of church growth books that offered the "real answer" to our church growth challenges:

The Turnaround Church

The Breakout Church

The Monday Morning Church

The Word and Power Church

The Disciple Making Church

The Organic Church

The Church That Works

The Missional Church

The Sticky Church (Really?)

And those were just the books that I saw on one shelf in my home library! My real library is at the university where I can wade through another ton of guaranteed solutions like: *The U Turn Church*, *The Un-Church*, and my all-time favorite title, *Simple Church*—two words that were never meant to go together!!!

Now, I have an explanation. I'm a practical theologian by profession, and church growth is my specialty area (that's my excuse and I'm sticking to it). Consequently, as a pastor, and now a trainer of pastors, I constantly find myself under a barrage of books that promise to answer all evangelism and church growth problems in a few simple steps. Don't believe it. Think diet books. They all promise a miracle. They all rarely work. They all have the same thing in common. If you exercise regularly, eat moderately and get plenty of rest—they work. What a surprise! Another victory for common sense.

Since 2012, Forbes Magazine and other media outlets have noted that the Adventist Church is the fastest growing church in America. A 2.5% growth rate is nothing to write home about, but it's clear that we are not the only group that's struggling to expand the kingdom. A number of reasons were cited to explain the growth. Our emphasis on health and simple living were cited, of course. But *USA Today* noted that one obvious reason was that a significant percentage of Adventist churches conducted revivals, reaping meetings or evangelistic campaigns during the calendar year. Now that's a thought. If you want to have a successful evangelistic campaign, you must conduct a campaign! Common Sense.

I am convinced that much of what we need to know about church growth can be observed by a 3rd grader working in a garden. Paul puts it this way in Galatians 6:7, we reap what we sow. Many televangelists have turned this text into a recipe for disaster, but it is a principle of life, and certainly a principle of church growth and evangelism. Jesus spoke about the growth of the kingdom in organic, agricultural terms. It you don't put anything in the ground, don't expect anything from the ground. Common sense. If there has been no real pre-work for the meeting, it will be a miracle if anything happens at the meeting. Common sense.

In other words, evangelism is a process that assumes that we will cultivate relationships, plant seeds of truth into those relationships, and then look for the harvest from those relationships. There are a number of programs and plans you can use. In fact, practically any legitimate church growth program will work—if you work it. But that's a blog for another day. Let's look at three common sense keys to church growth.

1. If it Ain't Broke—Don't Fix It!

Evangelism, like so many other ministries, can tend to follow the fad. At times, we seem to prefer the novel approach to the proven approach. If there is an approach to evangelism that is working for you, then work it. Don't change what you are doing just because someone commented that it wasn't contemporary.

Each pastor is made up of a unique blend of gifts, temperaments, and talents. We are all different. Our backgrounds and tastes are different. Our styles and strategies are different. When you find an evangelism strategy that works for you, there's probably a reason for it. It flows. It fits. And when you are comfortable, it makes others comfortable. People can sense when you are ministering in another man's armor.

Many traditional approaches to evangelism have been condemned to the trash heap. Tent evangelism and Revelation seminars, for example, are two approaches that have been criticized for being dated and ineffective. I must admit, I still have reoccurring nightmares of my early tent meetings. My tents blew down so often that storm clouds still make me break out in a cold sweat!

But in certain areas, tent evangelism works to this day. I still remember driving up Interstate 40 into Louisville, Kentucky and seeing a gigantic tent evangelistic meeting. The cars were everywhere! I was so amazed I stopped in myself. Whether it's novelty or nostalgia, if it works and it works for you—then work it. The same applies for Revelation Seminars. Some pastors have a natural teaching gift that's tailor made for that classroom approach. If it ain't broke, don't fix it.

2. If it Ain't Broke—It Will Be!

There is one thing that won't take any pastor long to learn. Few approaches to ministry or evangelism work forever. Attention spans are short. Interest levels are even shorter. Many a pastor has left the pulpit dejected because the sermon that worked on the road fell flat at home. Many an evangelist has left a campaign scratching his head because the series that baptized 50 in one place, only baptized 5 in another. There are a host of possible reasons for the difference, but this one thing is true: You have to be flexible and skilled enough to use multiple ministry and evangelistic approaches.

Ellen White is helpful here:

"God wants us all to have common sense, and He wants us to reason from common sense.

Circumstances alter conditions. Circumstances change the relation to things." [1]

Good stuff. Sharpen your skills. Add enough to your evangelistic and ministry toolbox to pull out another tool when the one you're using isn't working. Because what works extremely well this year might not work at all next year. It's one of the reasons that I have been encouraging leaders to take responsibility for their professional growth. Too many leaders are at an absolute loss when things begin to stall or break down in their ministries. It might very well be that the principles and programs that you learn at a conference this year might save your ministry next year.

3. If it Ain't Broke—Bend It.

I'm not a fan of soccer. No offense to the fans of the "beautiful game" but I prefer my football with shoulder pads. But like most Americans, I jumped on the World Cup bandwagon. I was impressed with Germany and even more interested when I read about their journey to the championship.

It seems that for decades the German national team was a force, but they experienced one heartbreaking loss after another in big matches. They were a model of efficiency, but couldn't quite seem to get over the hump. In June of 2004, after another disappointing loss in the European championship, the Germans made a major change that paved the way to their 2014 World Cup Championship victory. They revamped their program and prioritized the recruitment and development of young players. The youth movement revolutionized German soccer and the future seems bright for years to come.

The team went from good to great. They did it by making adjustments to a system that was already working but needed to work better. A wise leader knows how to make adjustments, to "bend" even the best system to keep it fresh for the future. Some of our evangelistic methods don't need to be discarded they just need to be adjusted.

A great example is Dr. Carlton Byrd, the pastor of the Oakwood University Church and director of Breath of Life television ministry. He is one the most productive evangelists in the church, but I call him the best of "old school." His meetings are a throwback to the best of traditional evangelism. From his legion of Bible workers, to his quiz cards, to his sermon titles, if you closed your eyes you might think you traveled back to an E. E. Cleveland campaign. However, his media, music, and marketing are as contemporary as the evening news.

And again, Ellen White reminds us, "Men are needed who pray to God for wisdom, and who, under the guidance of God, can put new life into the old methods of labor and can invent new plans and new methods of awakening the interest of church members and reaching the men and women of the world." [2]

Here's to common sense and growing churches.

---

[1] Selected Messages Book 3, p.217.
[2] Evangelism, p.105.

10

WHAT TO DO WHEN YOUR CHURCH IS DYING?

You remember the story? *"The Emperor Who Wore No Clothes."* It's a Hans Christian Anderson classic. Let me refresh your memory.

Many years ago, there was a king who was obsessed with his fine clothes. His greatest joy was showing them off to his subjects. One day, two crafty crooks convinced him that they could make him the finest suit of the world's most beautiful cloth. But there was something "special" about this suit, they said. It was invisible to anyone who was stupid…and some other conditions I forgot.

Well, the tricksters put the invisible suit on the king and he ignored his nakedness because that would prove, of course, that he was stupid. His friends claimed they could see the suit because they didn't want to be dumb either. The king put on his invisible suit and led a parade through the streets and everyone pretended that they could see a suit that wasn't there. Because if they didn't see the suit it would insult the king and worse yet, it would be a sign that they were stupid.

So, everyone praised the king for his magnificent suit. Until a little boy looked up and spoke up. "The King has nothing on!" "The Emperor has no clothes!" "He's naked as a jaybird" (Actually, I made that last one up.) No one wanted to admit the obvious.

Churches can be like that king. The signs of trouble can be everywhere, but the church limps along as if all is well. No two churches are alike, but the warning signs are strangely similar.

- Attendance has dropped drastically over the years.
- The average age of the members is way up.
- The neighborhood has drastically changed.
- There is more talk of the past than the future.
- The bills and the building are becoming harder to maintain.
- There are few visitors and even fewer new members.

Local churches are the apple of God's eye and healthy local churches are the hope of community. Let me list some suggestions for churches who are not satisfied with the shape that they are in.

Admit that there is a problem

It's impossible for God to fix a problem that we don't face. If you are a local member, have a quiet conversation with your pastor. If you are the pastor, have a conversation with a supportive, long-time member. Just an honest conversation among faithful members who want things to get better.

Pray!

Determine a time for prayer and fasting. It may be with a small group of interested members or it may be with the church body. Surveys and strategies alone will never solve the problem of a dying church.

Get some "outside eyes"

There are some things that only an outsider can really see. Churches have the remarkable ability to adapt to difficult situations and that's a good thing. But you can't correct what you can't see. And there are some things that a local pastor just can't say. It can be seen as self-serving or it may be suicidal. Bring in an objective outsider to help with the process.

Take a careful look at your history

What has happened in your recent or distant past? Some churches started for the wrong reasons. Other churches started at the wrong size. These historical decisions can have an ongoing impact on the condition of the local church. Evaluate the seasons of the church. When were things going well? When did the slide begin?

Take a hard look at the numbers

You don't want a doctor to give you false figures from your physical. You want the facts because they tell you the real shape that you're in. Same for the church. Look at the attendance and baptism numbers over a 4 or 5-year span. Look at the trends. Take another look at the financials. Look at the trends.

Take a realistic look at the location

This is one of the most consistent characteristics of struggling churches. The neighborhood has changed. What was once a neighborhood church, is now a commuter church. This could actually be a blessing in disguise, but that's not the question at this point. Does the membership reflect the neighborhood? Why or why not?

Take a loving look at the congregation

Who is actually attending church? What is the average age of the congregation? Are there conflicts that are inhibiting growth? Are there traditions that are limiting growth? Is there corruption that is killing growth? This is sensitive stuff and points up the need for prayer, patience, and wise counsel.

Recast the vision for what is actually there

At some point the church has to make a decision about the future. If the decision is to continue, then a vision for the future needs to be carefully cast. But it must be a realistic vision that doesn't just look at the future alone, but at the present condition and resources.

You probably won't attract millennials in large numbers to a church of senior citizens. You probably won't attract young couples to a church with nothing for their kids. Real vision comes from a real look at real circumstances.

Watch, Work, and Wait.

The church is too precious an organism to rush to any conclusions. After the problems have been determined and solutions suggested, it's time to go to work. Work, watch and wait. Come back at designated points to monitor progress. Some problems take time to solve. Some solutions take time to develop.

11

WHEN SHOULD WE CLOSE A LOCAL CHURCH?

It's a sensitive topic. It's an unpleasant reality. But many local churches seem to be dying right before our eyes. What was once a thriving center in a vibrant neighborhood is now a decaying island in a neighborhood long gone.

The signs are usually there. Some of them I mentioned in my blog, *"What to Do When Your Church Is Dying?"* and others can be found in works like Thom Rainer's, *"Autopsy of a Deceased Church."*

There has been no appreciable growth, numerically or financially, in more than five years. (Let's make it seven for the prophetic crowd.)

- The neighborhood around the church has drastically changed but the church has not.
- The average age of the membership has risen sharply.
- The bills and the building are becoming harder to maintain.
- The goal of the church has become survival and maintenance rather than mission.
- The membership is not willing to change.
- The membership is not willing to accept their responsibility for the decline.

All is not lost. There are very few churches who have not struggled with some or all of those characteristics at some point. Dying churches are regularly revived but not without great sacrifice. These are some of the general characteristics of churches that survive:

- A crisis arises that forces the local congregation to face its real condition.
- The church engages outside, objective counsel to work through the crisis.
- The church admits that it is in crisis.
- The church confronts the problems and persons who contribute to the crisis.
- A gifted local leader arises or is appointed and takes the church through a radical restoration process.

The church identifies a ministry or missional "niche" that allows it to make an ongoing contribution to the kingdom regardless of its size or age. Examples are: elder care ministries, social media ministries, child care ministries, legal aid ministries, Christian education ministries, etc.

But it seems to me that there is a point when some churches just need to be closed. Now, if you're looking for some biblical instructions for closing a church, you'll be disappointed. However, living organisms, and a church is a living organism, go through predictable life stages: birth, adolescence, adulthood, old age, and death.

I believe that's true of churches also. At some point the best of churches will crumble. Looking for Ephesus? You'll have to go on an archeological dig. Time will tumble some churches. Others are victims of geography. Some fall prey to apostasy.

There are many churches that have found ways to not only survive but thrive. Ultimately a church should be judged on its ability to fulfill the mission of the local church, which is to make disciples-developed and devoted followers of Christ. So, I believe we should consider closing local churches:

- When the local membership has not grown for 5-7 years and resists plans to change.
- When they refuse to submit to a thoughtful restoration process.
- When the local church is more successful at running souls off than bringing souls in.
- When other local churches are close enough to reach the souls the church in crisis refuses to reach.

Churches should be closed as a very last resort, but in some cases, they should be closed nonetheless.

Church closures can actually be the grain of wheat spoken of in John 12 that dies but then brings forth much fruit. Churches can combine their memberships and resources for greater impact. Churches can resource new church plants and continue to live in other locations. Some churches can stop their perpetual search for the sixties and do a new thing. Some churches can stop reminiscing about the glory days and begin to tell a whole new story.

It's a lot easier to talk about closing churches than it is to close them. Lives are impacted. Feelings are hurt. Hopes are dashed. But that's also a description of what's happening every week in many unhealthy churches.

"There is a time for everything, and a season for every activity under the heavens, a time to be born and a time to die..." - Ecclesiastes 3:1-2 NIV

12

CHICK-FIL-A: WHAT YOUR CHURCH COULD LEARN

Since 2010, Chick-fil-A has been the most successful fast food restaurant in America. It leads the fast food industry in sales per store by a large margin. Like most "overnight success stories," Chick-fil-A labored for more than 20 years before it opened its first store in the Greenbriar Mall in Atlanta. From there the explosion began.

Experts point to a number of reasons for the store's success. But the unmistakable force behind the popular franchise was the founder, S. Truett Cathy. Born in 1921, he was a picture of hard work and traditional values. (His critics would argue, too traditional.) For more than 50 years he was a Sunday School teacher at the First Baptist Church in Jonesboro, Arkansas. Not unlike a former Sunday School teaching peanut farmer in Plains, Georgia by the name of Jimmy Carter.

When Cathy died in 2014, Chick-fil-A was worth close to 3 billion dollars and he was one of the most generous philanthropists in American history. He was sought out by industries, governments, and universities worldwide for his counsel on business, stewardship and education.

But in the nineties, S. Truett Cathy unintentionally gave some counsel to the local church that's revolutionary.

After years of explosive growth, Chick-fil-A was facing pressure from a new kid on the block, Boston Market. The newcomer was in most of the same markets as Chick-fil-A and growing by leaps and bounds. Boston Market also announced huge expansion plans for the future. Chick-fil-A's corporate managers were shaken.

At a regular meeting of the board of trustees, one board member after another expressed concern. "We are still the market leaders, but Boston Market is closing fast" they complained. According to Andy Stanley who related this story in his leadership blog in 2013, everyone seemed to be saying the same thing. "We need to get bigger- faster! Bigger-faster! Bigger- Faster!"

S. Truett Cathy, who was usually the quiet presence in the board room, listened until he could take it no more. He pounded the desk until the room got quiet. And then he made this amazing statement.

"I am sick and tired of you talking about getting bigger! What we need to be talking about is getting BETTER! If we get better, our customers will demand that we get bigger!!"

Now that's a word! Not just a word for Chick-fil-A, but a valuable word for the local church. It is important for the church to get bigger. Despite the constant criticism, personal and public evangelism is not a numbers game. When we realize that those "numbers" represent our lost mothers and fathers and sons and daughters, we understand why Christ called the church to be more than faithful. The church must be fruitful. (Luke 13)

But you don't get bigger by obsessing over size. You get bigger by obsessing over substance. The church has to get better before it gets bigger. Better at what?

Better at the Gospel of Jesus Christ

The gospel is by definition the good news of what Jesus did to restore us to God. Broadly speaking the entire Bible contains the gospel, but not everything Is the gospel. At times, what seems to be missing from the "gospel," is Jesus. We are fairly comfortable with expressions of the gospel. Things like diet, education, and service. But I sense a need for a more specific understanding of what Jesus did and how that should influence our daily living. I say it often, but it's impossible to share the gospel if the good news is not good to you.

Better at making disciples

The great commission is to make disciples. Matthew 28. That's a lot different from making converts. Making baptisms. Our goal is a fully devoted follower of Jesus Christ. We have to bring them in, build them up, and then send them back out. It's a lifetime commitment that demands the full investment of the local church. If the local church is shallow here, as most churches seem to be, then the front door will rarely open and when it does- the back door will swing. In short, they'll go out as quickly as they come in.

Better at demonstrating love

I love the church. But at times it can be a mean, mad, unforgiving place. We should regularly remind ourselves that it's our love that distinguishes us as Christians. (John 13:35.) In my blog, *"What Do They See When We Say Adventist,"* I spoke of a word association game that I've played for years across the globe. "What word comes to mind when you hear Adventist?" I've never heard love. Clunky game? Sure. Does it illustrate a problem? Sure again.

S. Truett Cathy was right. If we focus on getting better, our customers will demand that we get bigger. The customers of the local church are the non-believers that surround the church building and the church members. That's great advice from a chicken salesman. It's probably no coincidence that the corporate purpose statement of Chick-fil-A is:

"To glorify God by being a faithful steward of all that is entrusted to us, and to have a positive influence on all who come into contact with Chick-fil-A."

Sounds like a church to me.

What can your local church learn from a chicken store?

Apparently, in the case of Chick-fil-A, quite a bit. I thought I was done with this story, but obviously there's still meat on the bones! (I know. I couldn't stop myself.)

It seems that there's no middle ground when Chick-fil-A comes up. People either love them or hate them. And the issue is not the food, which receives consistently great reviews. The issue is the statements that they've made about traditional values. The management's understanding of marriage being between a man and woman, is not exactly winning them friends today. And the fact that they've decided to close on Sundays has made them even more controversial.

But whether you agree with them or not, their success in the market and popular culture can't be argued. They are the most successful fast food restaurant in America by a long shot. They make more sales per store in 6 days than the others do in 7. So, what are they doing?

It begins with the founder, S. Truett Cathy. Last week I wrote of his challenge to the Chick-fil-A board of trustees who were obsessing over getting "bigger-faster!" His response to them was good advice for his business and even better advice for the local church. He said, "I am sick and tired of you talking about getting bigger. What we need to be talking about is getting better! If we get better, our customers will demand that we get bigger!"

I love it! Church ministries and church growth is what I do. I love bigger! But quantity without quality is a disaster in the making. Bringing new believers into some of our churches is like bringing babies into a nasty nursery. They won't be there long.

But what more can we learn from Chick-fil-A? Let's begin with the "Core Four" counsel that they give to all employees:

- *Make eye contact* – That works at a chicken store or at church. People who make eye contact are usually seen as more reliable, warm, and sociable.
- *Smile* – Enough said.
- *Speak enthusiastically* – Often it's not what you say but how you say it. Enthusiastic communication is persuasive communication.
- *Stay connected* – Chick-fil-A encourages their sales force to establish relationships with customers. The founder of the church encourages the same.

Great advice. However, the core four are only extensions of the five Core Values of Chick-fil-A. Here we pick up the key to their success and the best lessons for the local church.

Core Value Number One: Customers First

This is the foundation of good customer service. The customer might not always be right, but the customer is always first. Think of the visitors who leave local churches complaining that no one spoke to them or greeted them. It's cliché, but you don't get a second chance to make a first impression.

I remember being introduced to a local church when my family was young. While I was in the office with the conference president, preparing to come out, my wife had taken a seat with our babies. A long-time member came down the aisle prepared to sit in her usual seat, only to find my wife and kids "innocently" sitting in her seat.

Two people got embarrassed that day. My wife, when the lady told her that my family was in her seat. And the lady when she later realized that I was the new pastor…and the intruder was the new pastor's wife….and the kids were the new pastor's babies! Incidentally, my wife waited for over a year to tell me that story, because I get mad to this day when I think about it!

Core Value Number Two: Personal Excellence

Christians should be recognized for the quality of their work. This should be the case at church, but most importantly, at the workplace. The greatest witness to the power of Christianity in the workplace is an excellent Christian worker. Christians don't go to work to proselytize or to witness, but they go to work…to work! The excellence of their work should reflect the excellence of their God.

Paul put it this way, *"Whatever you do, work at it with all of your heart, as working for the Lord and not for human masters; since you know that you will receive an inheritance from the Lord as a reward..."* - Colossians 3:23-24 NIV

CORE VALUE NUMBER THREE: Continuous Improvement

Chick-fil-A calls it continuous improvement, the church calls it sanctification or Christian maturity. In the Christian life, we are either going forward or backward, but we're always moving. Ellen White reminds us of how important continuous improvement is:

"Our first responsibility toward God and our fellow beings is that of self-development." (Temperance pg. 137)

CORE VALUE NUMBER FOUR: Working Together

Resources are wasted, and talent is squandered when church members don't work together. In some churches, especially churches of size, the ministries and departments seem to operate as silos. Competition for resources and spots for "special days" can be fierce. Of course, this is a reflection of how little the members understand and own the primary mission of the church.

The church has been uniquely gifted for growth. Ephesians 4:11-16 states that each Christian has at least one gift and when those gifts operate together we are no longer children influenced by every shiny fad or face, but we grow into mature believers. This only happens when the church works together. Chick-fil-A is on point again.

CORE VALUE NUMBER FIVE: Stewardship

"To glorify God by being a faithful steward of all that is entrusted to us and to have a positive influence on all who come into contact with Chick-fil-A." That is the corporate purpose of Chick-fil-A. It should be the stewardship statement of every Christian.

That's it. For sure, churches and for-profit businesses are not the same. There are significant differences in mission, compensation, administration, and motivation. But there are certain things that the church just ought to do better than a chicken store!

13

A Martian, a Meeting, and the Mission

I was exercising in downtown Grand Rapids, Michigan, and the setting was nothing short of inspiring. The Gerald Ford Presidential Museum was to my left, the Michigan River was on my right, and I ran down a damp trail between them. My mind was racing through a church leadership workshop that I was scheduled to conduct later that morning. But then the strangest thought occurred to me.

Suppose an alien from outer space sat in on one of our church board meetings? (I told you it was strange.) Just go with me.

It seems that a Martian and his little green buddies have been visiting popular organizations on Earth to try to understand them. They have heard about this strange organization called a "church", so they send someone down to investigate. They want to understand the church. What makes it tick? What is its mission?

So, one little Martian parked next to the Pastor's spot and walked—I guess—into the church. He followed the voices into a pleasant room of about twenty people all seated around a big table. Most of them were so deep in their discussion that they barely looked up as the visitor came in. He knew enough English to understand a white-haired lady when she whispered, "He looks kinda strange. Must be from the Conference Office." That must have been the general sentiment because the Martian was allowed to sit down without incident.

So, there he sat, the Martian in the church board meeting. And he tried to determine what business the church was in by the conversations around the table.

First, they plunged into a lengthy discussion about the budget and church finances. The Martian thought, "They must be a banking or lending institution of some sort."

Then the conversation shifted to an animated discussion about something called Adventurers and Pathfinders. The Martian decided the church had to be like the Boy Scouts and Girl Scouts of America that they had observed in an earlier visit.

The Church School discussion had the Martian totally confused. The notes he took read, "I was wrong! It's an educational institution."

One discussion got so heated that the little fellow scribbled with excitement, "I think I got it. Fighting! It's a strange kind of fighting that they do." But then the focus shifted again, and the Martian was back to square one.

As the conversation shifted from musicals to retreats to potlucks, the Martian seemed further and further from discovering the primary mission of the church. Finally, he slipped out of the room, into his spaceship and headed home.

"So, what did you find?", they asked as he opened up his report. *"What was the mission of the church? What do they actually do?"*

"Well, I'm not quite sure," he said. "They talked about a lot of things. They all seemed important, but nothing seemed to really drive the conversation. Nothing really stood out."

By that time, an older Martian spoke up. He was a veteran in the Mission to Earth project and he had listened with interest to the report.

"Interesting! So, you say you heard the church members speaking about a number of things: Pathfinders, potlucks, Christian education, General Conference…"

"Yes…That's right."

"Well I'm pretty sure that the primary instructions of the originator of the church was that they were to go and make disciples—whatever that means," the veteran Martian said. "Seeking and saving the lost, I think I heard him say."

"In fact, those were the last instructions he gave them before he disappeared."

"Nope. That's not it," the little green guy mumbled. "I'm pretty sure I didn't hear that…at all."

14

How Adventist Evangelism, Hurts Adventist Evangelism

We have a problem. It's a big problem. Let me illustrate it this way. The average life expectancy for a US citizen is 78.7 years. For men, it's 76 years. For women, it's 81 years. I could speculate about the reason for the difference, but my wife reads my blog, so I won't!

Now, it is alleged that by the time most Christians come to the end of life, they would have:

- *Heard 5,000 sermons*
- *Sung 10,000 songs*
- *Prayed 20,000 prayers*
- *Led **no one** to Christ*

That illustration has obvious flaws. There are holes in the math, differences in circumstances and various definitions of soul winning. But it begs an important question. How many Christians can recall one person they personally led to Christ? What about *you*?

There are numerous challenges to effective evangelism; neglected prayer, outdated methods, lack of divine power, the list goes on. But let's look at three challenges to our traditional evangelism practices.

Adventist Evangelism Hurts Adventist Evangelism:

When Methods Are Unchanged

It's obvious why some evangelistic ideas and efforts are unfruitful. The calendar has changed, but the methods are the same. Going to the evangelistic campaign is like taking a nice stroll down memory lane. There's not a thing wrong with that if people are responding, and needs are being met. I don't believe in innovation for the sake of innovation, but if the horse is dead, it's time to dismount.

"Let every worker in the Master's vineyard, study, plan, and devise methods, to reach the people where they are. We must do something out of the common course of things." [1] I agree with Ellen White. We need to respect tried and true principles. But the definition of insanity is to continue to do the same thing and expect a different result.

When Ministers Are Unchallenged

In another life, I was the Director of Church Growth and Discipleship for a large conference. Early on I discovered that 37 churches had not baptized a single person in three years. Not good for an institution whose mission is to baptize and make disciples (Matt. 28). But my biggest surprise came when I spoke to the pastors. Most of them had no clue that it had been so long between baptisms. Each situation was unique and there was no quick fix, but I noticed that the ministers responded well when I challenged them through accountability and continuing education.

Accountability

I believe in accountability. Ministers need it, and churches need it too. I don't think you reach your potential without it. Accountability at its best is redemptive and instructive. It helps you know what condition you are in. In the same way that a doctor gives you a "count" of your blood pressure, cholesterol and other vitals at a physical, accountability helps leaders know how healthy they are. Ministers and churches need to know how well they are doing in the work of building God's kingdom.

Continuing Education

Most of us stop learning too soon. For many ministers, their exposure to new ideas and methods stops at the seminary. Continuing education exposes ministers to approaches that will help reach a world that is changing at warp speed. There will always be church members who are reluctant to support anything that the Adventist church didn't baptize, or Pacific Press didn't publish. That can be a blessing in disguise. It forces deep thought and discernment. But if you are a minister, continue to pursue the best resources inside and outside the denomination.

When Members Are Uninvolved

There is one thing that I find missing from most Adventist meetings...The Adventists! It seems that members are largely uninterested and uninvolved in their own evangelistic meetings. Most ministers seem to put forward a strong effort to get members involved, but the results are inconsistent. And when members are not involved in public evangelism, it's harder to reach people and keep people.

Harder to reach people

Charles and Win Arn conducted an important survey. They determined after surveying over 14,000 people that most Christians come to Christ or a church because of a friend or relative. Not because of an evangelist or online bible study, but because of a friend, a loved one, a member. If members are not connecting their friends to Christ, then it's not likely that a flyer or television broadcast will replace their efforts.

Harder to keep people

The best way to keep the people from coming in the front door of the church and leaving out the back, is for them to have relationships in the church. Period.

So, What Do We Do?

We will return to this subject often, but to keep well-meaning evangelism fresh and effective we should consider this. We should give evangelism a new meaning, a new location and a secret weapon.

It would be helpful to think of the word "witness" when we see the word evangelist. That's a little closer to what God expects of us. God doesn't expect each of us to be full-time bible instructors or conference evangelists, but according to Acts 1:8, he does expect us to be witnesses. In fact, he has already given you, not only the power to witness, but the location and a secret weapon.

Your location to witness is right where you are. Before you take a mission trip across the seas take a walk across the street or across the room. That's your primary mission field. And your secret weapon is your life experience.

"Far more than we do, we need to speak of the precious chapters in our experience. No more effective means can be employed for winning souls to Christ." [2]

God uses your life experiences–good and bad–to attract men and women to the cross. When they see how God works through the lives of real people, it moves them in a strange way, a supernatural way.

So, let's get off the sidelines and into the game. God has already provided everything we need to make evangelism work.

---

[1] E.G. White, Letter 20, 1893
[2] E.G. White, *Christ's Object Lessons*, p. 299

Worship

15

SEVEN REASONS CHURCHES DON'T SING

At first, I thought it was just me, but I soon found out it's not. Churches just don't seem to be singing as much as they once did.

By singing I mean congregational singing. I'm in a different church every month, sometimes every week. It's what I do. I work with churches. And one of the complaints that I hear from pastors and worship leaders alike is, "These folks just don't want to sing!"

Now you would think that getting the congregation to sing would never be a problem these days. Why? Because everybody has a praise team. By everybody I mean…everybody!

A church is evidently not a church without a praise team. Even if the church is so small that the church *is* the praise team, they still have a praise team!

Now I love music, and in another life, I sang, directed choirs and led praise teams. I also pastored for more years than I care to remember with music departments large and small. So, let me offer seven nonscientific, unsolicited, but certainly familiar reasons that many churches don't sing!

CHURCHES DON'T SING

1. Because the song leader is not singing! Well, what is he doing? He's ministering. What's ministering? Well, we used to call it talking, but evidently, when you are a praise team leader it's called ministering. Whatever you call it, it's not singing, and it would help if that's what a singer would do. Nothing kills a congregational song like a leader who talks too much.

2. Because they don't know the songs. Familiarity is a song leader's best friend. It's no accident that churches immediately respond when a familiar song is sung. There is nothing wrong with new material, but teach it. And don't assume that because you taught it last week, they know it this week. Teach it and teach it again.

3. Because they want a hymn! Now let me be clear. I'm to the left of most people when it comes to religious music. I love contemporary gospel music, and for me, the longer and the louder, the better. That's just me. But wake me up in the middle of the night and I could sing all 5 verses of practically any hymn…and probably give you the number in the hymnal as well. I love hymns, and I'm not alone.

There is nothing like a hymn. Praise and worship songs are great. They generally express an intimacy that's important to our relationship with God. But the lyrical content of hymns gives them staying power. Not only do we need them, but we need more of them. Not just old hymns, but new hymns, by new writers, with new sensibilities.

4. Because the songs are too complicated. Now I have a terminal degree. I teach at a great university. I'm a Doctor! But at times I'm totally lost trying to learn some of these songs and sing them at the same time. Especially with multiple verses and crazy chords and strange syncopation…you get the picture. Keep it simple.

5. Because the music is too loud. I said it earlier. I like loud music. You can't listen to James Hall and Vashawn Mitchell and the folk I listen to without cranking it up. But volume totally loses its impact when it's loud all the time. I attended a service recently and the children were leading out. No, actually, the **band** was leading out, because they were all we could hear. The parents were not pleased, and neither was the congregation.

6. Because they feel manipulated. I have led praise and worship for years and I know the frustration of getting a church to sing. I also know that certain clichés and phrases and even scriptures really work to get people involved. But there is a thin line between motivation and manipulation.

Eventually, the tricks and clichés don't work. Here's a favorite. "If you were at a football game you'd be on your feet shouting for your favorite team. Well, we serve a God who deserves our best praise..." Really? Well, that's true, but we're not at a football game! And if I were at a football game I'd have a hotdog and popcorn. Did I miss that on the way into the sanctuary? And for the record, if I were at a football game, I wouldn't be standing as long as you have me standing in this praise and worship set!

You get the picture. The point is manipulation is lazy and actually unnecessary for a people who have received so much from God. The song leader's job is to creatively remind them of who God is. John 12:32 is still true, *"And I, if I be lifted up from the earth, will draw all men unto me."*

7. Because they need to love the God they sing about. This is a much more complicated issue. It actually has more to do with what goes on before the service than the service itself. But at times music can lift people to places that a sermon can't take them. So, leaders should take seriously their roles as living instruments in the hands of God.

So, pastors, choir directors, praise team leaders, let's take up the challenge to encourage our congregations to worship a God who deserves much more than a song!

16

THREE MORE REASONS CHURCHES DON'T SING

Some subjects touch a nerve. I'm pretty sure this one hit an artery! The discussion went on for days. In my blog entitled, *"Seven Reasons That Churches Don't Sing,"* the seven reasons we explored were:

1. Because the song leader is not singing.
2. Because they don't know the songs.
3. Because they want a hymn.
4. Because the songs are too complicated.
5. Because the music is too loud.
6. Because they feel manipulated.
7. Because we need to love the God we sing about.

Now, I noticed that much of the discussion about congregational singing last week had a generational slant to it. I understand. I grew up in the 60s and 70s, B.P.T. (Before Praise Teams). On Saturday mornings in churches everywhere, there was a chorister who led the morning hymn. On Sunday morning an old, and I do mean old, deacon led out the devotion at the Baptist church. And over at Temple of Deliverance, a "mother" armed only with a tambourine, was wrecking the house.

Well, a number of things have changed since those days. Some good and some bad. However, the result seems to be less congregational singing. So, let's look at three more unscientific but undeniable reasons that some churches don't sing.

1. Because the songs are in a bad key.

A bad key can hurt a good song. I remember growing up hearing one person after another die a slow painful death singing, *"He Looked Beyond My Faults"* (Amazing Grace). You know the song, "Amazing grace, shall always be my song of praise…" Now for me, as soon as I heard the first note, I knew that when they got to "How Marvelous!", somebody was going to be laughing! (I'm not proud of myself.) Correct keys are absolutely critical.

Certain worship songs and hymns demand to be transposed. While I was writing this blog, I got a text from my absolute favorite pianist of all time, Gale Jones Murphy. We grew up singing and worshipping together in Memphis. She reminded me that the hymnal that most Adventist churches use was published in 1985. The older hymnal that we grew up with had (generally) higher keys. That could be a problem.

The point is this, I'm not a musician, but when the church is singing, and the men are switching octaves, straining necks, and sweating bullets – it's time to change the key.

2. Because the singers or musicians are unprepared.

Singers and musicians are gifts to the body of Christ. They can frankly make or break a worship service. That's probably why the Bible puts such emphasis on musicians and worship leaders being skilled (see 1 Chronicles 15:22; 25:7).

Now skill doesn't make our worship more acceptable to God, but it does demonstrate that we appreciate the gift. Musical skill in the local church is generally a combination of spiritual gift and discipline. One without the other is a problem. And the older I get the more I favor discipline over natural or even spiritual gift. Because I've seen too many gifted folks accomplish very little because they won't practice.

When singers and musicians are unprepared they can be tentative and unsure. It hampers their service. It can literally keep the congregation from experiencing congregational singing and worship at its fullest.

3. Because congregational singing is not a priority

People can tell what we value. We prioritize it. We emphasize it. We invest in it. If we want our churches to sing, then our local churches need to make congregational singing a priority. The ways to do that are limited only by our imaginations. Praise teams can be sensitive to some of the principles previously discussed.

 Churches can invest in continuing education, conferences, and workshops for musicians and worship leaders. Put your money where your mouth is.

Some churches might want to bring back the hymn of the morning and even purchase new hymnals.

Church leaders who are on the platform during worship should always participate in congregational singing.

Unless the song is super-simple or familiar to all, the lyrics should be available for all to see.

The pastor is the key. He or she can teach the value of congregational singing and encourage the church to sing. But most importantly, the pastor can provide an example by joining the congregation in song.

Finally, let me repeat myself. The issue for the church is not the praise team, soloists, choirs nor congregational singing. They are all marvelous means of expression and worship. They all have their strengths and limitations, but ultimately the same rule should apply to each of them. We would see Jesus!

17
EVERYTHING THAT SHOUTS AIN'T PENTECOSTAL

It's the word that strikes fear in the hearts of countless Adventists…

Pentecostal!

It inspires images of everything from holy dancing to holy flesh. From speaking in tongues to slaying in the Spirit. It's the first complaint many conference presidents hear on their way in, and the last complaint many pastors hear on their way out!

You've probably heard the criticism.

"That service was entirely too Pentecostal," or "too Baptist", or my all-time favorite, "too first-day."

Then there is the classic, "This is an *Adventist* church!"

These days the villain of choice is, "neo-Pentecostalism." That label alone can shut down a discussion. Some presenters toss the term around like a torpedo, and you sense they searched for sources to validate an opinion they already had. Their purpose is generally to warn about worship they have judged to be inappropriate or unbiblical.

Classic Pentecostalism is a renewal movement within the Protestant church that began well over a century ago. Today, there are more than 700 Pentecostal denominations, with no central structure but a fairly consistent belief system.

Growing up in Memphis, Tennessee, I lived in the shadow of the largest Pentecostal denomination in the world, the Church of God in Christ. Back then I was always struck by how similar they were to Adventists in certain areas:

Conservative Protestant Theology

Pentecostal evangelists, like Adventist preachers, were railing against the danger of liberal theology. They preached the second coming of Jesus, the authority of the Scriptures, the Trinity, the literal resurrection of Jesus, salvation by grace alone, etc.

Separated Living

Pentecostals gave a whole new meaning to the word, "holiness." As strict as Adventists were, they were in good company with Pentecostals who preached against everything from motion pictures to baseball; from lipstick to sheer stockings, long hair on men to short hair on women. They were tough.

"Sabbath" Observance

Now the day was different, but the restrictions were absolutely the same. No cooking on Sunday. No washing on Sunday. No TV on Sunday. No bike riding on Sunday. Nothing but church, church and when you finished with that...more church!

Of course, the distinction that causes the controversy is the Pentecostal emphasis on the works of the Holy Spirit. Particularly their emphasis on the baptism of the Spirit with the evidence of speaking in tongues. This emphasis on experiencing the "fullness" of the Spirit has inspired a generation of enthusiastic worship and a flood of destructive theology.

It's important not to paint all lively worship services with a broad, "neo-Pentecostal" brush. Contexts are different. Things change. For instance, growing up, drums were the devil's instrument. Which is interesting because years earlier the guitar was the devil's instrument. Years earlier it was the flute. Earlier still, it was the piano. Christian history is a must read.

My counsel is to get biblical before you get critical. And frankly, Seventh-day Adventists, with our proud history of visions and dreams and passionate worship services, should be especially humble when evaluating the worship of other faith traditions. Ellen White gives us a glimpse.

The place was filled with the Spirit of the Lord. Some rejoiced, others wept. All felt that the Lord was drawing very near…When seated Mrs. White began to praise the Lord, till her voice changed, and the deep clear shouts of Hallelujah thrilled every heart." [1]

"The influence of the melody, accompanied by Brother Clark's solemn appearance and sweet shouts seemed electrifying," White recalled. "Many were in tears, while responses of Amen and Praise the Lord were heard from almost everyone who loved the Advent hope." [2]

"I saw that singing to the glory of God often drove the enemy, and shouting would beat him back and give us victory." [3]

Students of Adventist history understand that enthusiasm in Adventist worship has ebbed and flowed as false movements came and went. Our priority is to always be a people of the book. That assumes that we'll be careful students of interpretation and context.

It helps to observe worship expressions that the Bible not only includes but also encourages.

> *Standing* – Psalm 119:120
>
> *Clapping* – Psalm 47:1
>
> *Lifting hands* – Psalm 63:4
>
> *Bowing* – Psalm 95:6
>
> *Shouting* – Psalm 27:6

I could have listed dancing, but I don't want to start a fight. *(That's actually not true. Good fights can be productive.)* My point is not to say that these expressions are appropriate in all places, at all times. But I am saying that they are appropriate in some places, at some times.

That's why I love worship at PELC. There's a lot of room between our seats and the stage! We're fine with a hearty amen or a silent witness. We might be in our thoughts, or on our faces, or on our feet. God has been just that good.

---

[1] James White, "Report of Meetings" Review and Herald, Oct. 22, 1857, pp. 196,197

[2] James White, "Life Incidents" p.107

[3] Ellen White to Arabella Hastings, Aug. 4, 1850 (letter 8,1850)

ADVENTIST ISSUES

18

THREE REASONS ADVENTISTS SHOULD CELEBRATE EASTER

Where will you be Sunday morning? In a few hours, Adventists across the country will enjoy an April weekend. On Sunday we'll be shopping in malls, watching the NBA playoffs with friends, or perhaps just relaxing at home. We'll probably be everywhere but where we should be – somewhere celebrating the resurrection of Jesus…Celebrating Easter.

Now, I get it. I'm writing this from a glass house. At this very moment, I'm preparing for alumni weekend on our university campus. Thousands will be here. Saturday will be a full day of worship and Christ will be at the center of it all. We may mention Easter somewhere along the way. Maybe not. That's not good enough.

Easter deserves special, undivided attention. Easter is one of the few days on the calendar that grabs the attention of Christians and non-Christians alike. Despite all the commercialism and confusion, Easter is a day that celebrates the resurrection of Jesus Christ. That alone is reason enough for Seventh-day Adventists to celebrate Easter. Here's why:

"Of all professing Christians, Seventh-day Adventists should be foremost in uplifting Christ." (Ellen White, *Evangelism* p. 188)

As imperfect as the holiday is, it's an opportunity to lift up Jesus. And frankly, Adventists are internationally known for a lot of things, but lifting up Jesus is not one of them. The resurrection that Easter celebrates is also especially meaningful because it's a foundation of our faith. Paul puts it this way.

"And if Christ has not been raised, then all our preaching is useless, and your faith is useless." – I Corinthians 15:14

So, let me give you three reasons that Adventists should celebrate Easter.

NUMBER ONE: We should celebrate Easter because it's not about the day but the Daystar!

The problem with Easter is the stuff that distracts: Easter bunnies, Easter eggs, Easter parades and Easter fashion. And for some Adventists, the biggest distraction is that it's celebrated on Sunday. They miss the irony of criticizing Christians for celebrating the resurrection on the day that Christ was resurrected. Go figure. But don't be distracted. The main attraction of Easter is Jesus and His resurrection. Everything else is secondary at best.

And please spare me the "pagan origins" of Easter arguments. If we go down that road, let's stop at the pagan origin of the names of weekdays and months, church steeples and clergy robes, wedding rings and flowers at funerals. And don't forget money. Surely, you've noticed the pagan symbols on some of our currency? So, in the spirit of Christian brotherhood, I'll hold your money while you work through these issues. You're welcome. Point is, lift up Jesus.

NUMBER TWO: We should celebrate Easter because we need to fellowship with other faiths.

There are not many opportunities for different faith traditions to get together without a fight. We generally emphasize our differences. Adventists need a reminder of how much we have in common with other Evangelical Christians. With certain obvious exceptions, we agree in most areas of doctrine with most mainline Christian denominations. In fact, historically and theologically, Adventists are about as close to the Methodist church as another denomination can get.

Here's the thing. Easter Sunday is a great time for Christians of all faiths to focus on the thing they have in common – their appreciation for the sacrifice of Jesus Christ and His resurrection. Fellowship and friendship lead to dialogue. Honest dialogue is what we need to understand and respect the beliefs of others and to share what we believe.

Side note: if the idea of worshipping with other believers is a significant issue with you, then my first advice is don't go and don't judge. My second advice is, grow up. You're not real light if no one sees you. You're not real salt unless you're mingling. No contact, no impact.

NUMBER THREE: We should celebrate Easter because a Resurrected God can resurrect YOU!

"But Christ has indeed been raised from the dead, the firstfruits of those who have fallen asleep. For since death came through a man, the resurrection of the dead comes also through a man. For as in Adam all men die, so in Christ all will be made alive" – 1 Corinthians 15:20-22 NIV

I just walked in from a funeral of a friend, Dr. Jonathan Thompson. Few men have left a clearer mark on their generation. We just spoke together a few days ago, and now he's gone. And that story is played out everywhere, every day. The resurrection promises victory over the death.

But the resurrection also promises power while we live. Romans 8 says that the same power that raised Jesus from the dead can live inside of us. That's real power. Resurrection power.

- Power to resurrect our broken lives.
- Power to resurrect our messed-up marriages.
- Power to resurrect our frustrated dreams.
- Power to resurrect our wasted gifts and talents.

That's the real meaning of Easter. It's another chance to say, "I need you", or "I thank you." It would be great to say that with other believers, but that's not a deal breaker. Find a way to celebrate Easter that works best for you. It may be in a church or in your secret place, but don't miss this chance to celebrate the Risen Savior. He lives!

19

TRICK OR TREAT! SHOULD CHRISTIANS CELEBRATE HALLOWEEN?

It's literally impossible to avoid Halloween these days. On that day, everyone from Donald Trump to Pennywise the Clown will be knocking on our doors looking for candy. There will be parties and movies and fright nights in the woods, and haunted houses. The celebration seems to have expanded from a single day to an entire month.

According to the National Retail Federation, almost 70% of Americans will be celebrating Halloween this year. It is second only to Christmas as a commercial holiday. A quarter of all of the candy sold this year will be sold this season. And adults across the country will be eating that same candy for months. Americans will spend over 8 billion dollars during this Halloween season. That's billion with a B!

THE ORIGIN

Where did Halloween come from? It seems that the celebration actually began with the Christian church. As early as the 4th century, according to church historian John Chrysostom, the church celebrated a festival in honor of martyred saints. It was called All Saints Day and originally held in May. The day before All Saints Day was called All Hallows(Holy) Day and eventually morphed into All Hallow E'en and eventually Halloween. Pope Gregory 4 shifted the original All Saints Day to November 1 to combat the popularity of the pagan Samhain Festival, and the rest is history.

THE ISSUE

So now the issue is, should Christians celebrate a pagan festival, or at least a festival with pagan origins? It's a good question. Halloween is circled on the calendar of the occult community. During the Halloween season:

- There will be countless attempts to contact the dead.
- More spells will be cast than at any other time of the year.
- Animal shelters will refuse to offer black cats for adoption for fear they will be used in a bloody sacrifice.

It is the pagan high and holy day. Nothing else comes close. How should a Christian handle Halloween? Here are some thoughts.

What about Christmas and Easter? Jesus wasn't born on December 25 and there were no eggs and bunnies at Calvary. Both of these celebrations have pagan origins, but Christians have chosen to infuse them with spiritual meaning. Of course, Halloween is worse. But if you're going to use pagan origins as your argument against Halloween, at least be consistent.

And don't stop with Halloween and Christmas and Easter. If you're having problems with pagan origins, you'll have problems with the names of weekdays and months, church steeples, clergy robes, wedding bands, and even flowers at funerals. And don't forget about those pagan symbols on our currency, or money. Just saying.

It's a matter of conscience – What does the Bible say about celebrating Halloween? Nothing specifically, but a lot in principle. Leviticus 20:27 and Deuteronomy 18:9-13 are among a number of passages that warn Christians about the danger of flirting with the occult. Many Christians quickly respond that they are not celebrating the Kingdom of darkness, and that they are not impacted or impressed by the history. Halloween seems to fall under the banner of disputable matters, Romans 14. Matters that good Christians can disagree on.

It reminds me of Paul's response to a disputable matter in I Corinthians 8. Jewish Christians were upset because Gentile Christians were eating meat that had been sacrificed to idols. (Sounds kind of Halloweenish to me.) It was causing such a stir in the church that Paul's eventual advice to the members was to stop it. It wasn't worth the trouble.

But Paul described the Jewish Christians as immature. "Weak' is the word he used. The idol, he reminded them, was nothing but a piece of stone. No matter what the original idol worshippers intended, that idol is "nothing", he says. He makes the point that if your conscious is bothered because of the origin and history of the meat, then it's wrong for you to eat it. But if another Christian has none of those issues with the meat, he's free to eat it. Seems like good counsel for Christians who don't see eye to eye on Halloween.

Don't celebrate like a pagan. If you choose to celebrate on Halloween, be careful how you do it. As I said earlier, Halloween is a high and "holy" day for the occult community. Each year around this time I receive a number of articles from former witches and warlocks who caution Christians not to be naïve about the spiritual and physical dangers of Halloween.

The Devil is real and so are his followers. Christians partying as demons and vampires are out of place any time of the year.

Christians celebrating inappropriately or to excess are wrong any time of the year. Christians entertaining themselves with occult books, and motion pictures, and television series are playing with fire any time of the year. It is absolutely wrong to celebrate Halloween as a pagan tribute to the kingdom of darkness.

Take the day back! Halloween actually has its roots in the church. It began with good intentions, but the Devil absolutely defiled it. Ephesians 5:11 says, "Have nothing to do with the fruitless deeds of darkness, but rather, Expose Them." One of the most powerful reasons for Christians to celebrate on Halloween is to expose the tricks of the Devil.

Halloween, with all of its baggage, is a great teachable moment. It's an opportunity to expose the Devil and his devices. So instead of screaming at the dark this Halloween, turn on the light. How?

Sponsor a Harvest Festival. Have a Halloween replacement celebration at your home or local church. Make sure that there are plenty of "treats" that will make the kids forget what they might be getting at a stranger's door. Some churches encourage the kids to come to these events as Bible characters and they have contests for the best custom. Be creative. Get the kids involved in the planning.

Have a brief but inspiring message. Teach the kids that there is literally a Great Controversy raging between the kingdom of God and the kingdom of Satan. Teach the kids that life with Christ is a life of power over darkness. I John 4:4. Bring in an age-appropriate speaker who can connect with the kids or go to the Christian bookstore and choose from a number of powerful videos and resources for just that purpose.

Create a space for creative Christian fun. This isn't rocket science. This isn't brain surgery. Many Christian kids are already disappointed that they are missing one of the most enjoyable days on their school calendar. They already feel a bit awkward explaining why they don't celebrate Halloween like their classmates. That's understandable. But it seems inexcusable for a local church to make a challenging holiday even worse by not scheduling some good clean Christian fun.

Halloween will always be a hot topic with Christians. It's one of those issues that will never be settled, but it's too important an issue not to discuss. I think the answer is this. Don't celebrate Halloween, but celebrate on Halloween. But that's me.

20

CAMP MEETINGS: HERE TO STAY OR TIME TO GO?

Please don't tell my Mother about this article. The title alone is enough to make me lose my spot at the holiday dinner table. I'm pretty sure that the 11th commandment for my mother and her pals is, *"Thou shalt not miss camp meeting."*

Camp meetings have been a part of the American landscape since the early 1800s. At the 1868 General Conference session in Battle Creek a vote was taken to endorse camp meetings for all Adventist conferences. From that point camp meetings have been a permanent part of Adventist church culture.

But there's a problem. My mother is a feisty, 80-year-old and that seems to be the average age of camp meeting attendees in many conferences. That's an exaggeration but not by much. A common observation of camp meetings across the country is that there are two prominent groups attending camp meeting these days. Senior citizens and the grandkids of said senior citizens. It's not a criticism it's an observation.

And the age of the camp meeting attendees isn't the only thing that's growing. So is the cost of camp meeting. No two conferences are alike. Their income is different. Their expenses are different. But if your conference is conducting a full camp meeting, they are probably spending anywhere from $200,000 to $750,000, depending on the size of the conference and workforce. Again, not a criticism but an observation.

Now, I happen to see huge possibilities whenever Christians gather in large numbers. The potential for vision casting, fundraising, and real revival is always there. But I think it's fair to expect conferences to carefully evaluate anything on their calendar or in their budgets as large as camp meeting. At the risk of oversimplifying, I suggest that they start by asking at least 3 questions.

What is the purpose?

What is the purpose of camp meeting? Now I have to warn you. If you are searching for a single purpose for all camp meetings, you'll be disappointed. Ellen White's statements about the purpose of camp meetings are a good example.

"Our camp meetings have another object…they are to promote spiritual life among our people. We meet to receive the divine touch." (Test. Vol. 6 pg. 32)

"The camp-meeting is one of the most important agencies in our work. It is one of the most effective methods of arresting the attention of the people, and reaching all classes with the gospel invitation… They should be held in the large cities and towns where the message of truth has not been proclaimed." (Gospel Workers pg. 400)

"A mistake has been made in holding camp-meetings in out-of-the-way places, and in continuing in the same place year after year." (Ibid)

So, is the purpose of camp meeting outreach or nurture? Should we be in large cities or small towns? Is our target audience new believers, non-believers, or mature believers? The answer to each of those options is probably yes. You can make a strong case for each option, depending on who you are and where you are, and when you are. But the point is make the case. Have the discussion.

What is the price?

I'm not suggesting that money should have the last word in the conversation about camp meeting, but it should speak up! I'm also not suggesting that camp meetings should be expected to carry their own weight financially. But I am suggesting that the price of camp meeting should reflect and enhance the priorities of the conference.

For instance, the Lake Region Conference has been blessed with forward thinking leadership. I watched as Dr. Cliff Jones and his executive committee slowly developed and communicated the conference's core values: Word, Worship, Wholeness and Witness. Each level of the conference was involved for maximum ownership. Conference goals and objectives flow out of these values. Camp meeting can be a perfect forum to regularly communicate and carry out those values and goals. If it does, for me it's worth the price.

Where are the people?

The fact that many camp meeting sites are practically empty during the week and full on the weekends says a lot. To some it says that people are not as spiritual or as committed as they once were. Maybe. It might be saying something totally different. It might be saying it's time for a change.

Camp meetings were birthed out of a need for flexibility and innovation. In the 1800s there were few churches on the frontier and even fewer pastors. The solution was to bring the people to the preacher rather than the preacher to the people. They innovated, and it worked.

Adventist camp meetings grew in large part because the Adventist message was unpopular in many areas and the churches and halls refused to rent to them. So, they gathered in the open air and in tents. They actually saved money and their numbers grew. They innovated, and it worked.

By observing the patterns of people, conferences can learn a lot about their priorities and needs.

I've said a lot. What do you think? Camp meetings. Here to stay or time to go?

21

PELC Preachers, Stay Off the Stage

If you love good preaching the Pastoral Evangelism and Leadership Council (PELC), is the place to be.

The training is excellent, the music is superb, the fellowship is fantastic, but the preaching is amazing. For 38 years preachers like Charles Brooks, Charles Adams, Gardner Taylor and Walter Pearson have blessed us. And recently William Curtis, Myron Edmonds, Lance Watson, Wesley Knight, Rudolph McKissick and others have set the place on fire.

This year, December 3-6, will be no exception with Freddie Haynes, Keith Morris, Roger Bernard, Gina Spivey Brown, Debleaire Snell, Cedric Belcher and Claybon Lea. And the young bucks, Dewaine Frazer and Ricardo Delahaye are going to light up the 5pm service. Which leads me to my subject.

Our 5pm service was in the Moseley Chapel. We highlight our newer generation there. The creativity is striking, and the energy is high. Now, traditional black preaching is a dialogue. At PELC, when we're not preaching, we're generally "helping the preacher" preach. Last year the preachers were a little too helpful for some when they literally came on the platform to "help the preacher." Of course, I wouldn't dare mention the name of the preacher who caused the most "trouble" in the Moseley Chapel…Gamal Alexander.

Now I gotta be honest. I loved it. Maybe not the brothers blocking my view on the platform, but the preaching and the response. I love the fact that worshippers at our services are comfortable enough to shout for joy or openly weep at the altar. I love the fact that every year the poinsettias in our evening services get taller and taller. (Inside joke. Ask a PELC pastor.)

PELC is primarily a pastor's conference. Pastors are a strange breed with an impossible job. They come to PELC not only for continuing education, but also for encouragement and fellowship, and frankly…hope. The magnitude of it all often comes to a head in the preaching services, which at times are as much therapeutic as they are spiritual. The 5pm service is particularly suited for those dynamics. It's more intimate. It's more informal. It's more personal.

But to be sure, you can have too much of a good thing. And it's generally not ok to come on the actual platform while the preacher is preaching. To be clear, I'm not speaking of platform participants but people coming up from the audience. Let me give you 3 reasons to stay off the stage.

It can be unsafe.

No one enjoys preaching more than me. I'm regularly attending services and conferences across the denominational spectrum. I love all genres and styles, but I have a particular love for traditional black preaching. It's not uncommon in many black services for people to be on their feet, hands lifted, voices raised, and consciously or unconsciously moving toward the preacher. But to actually mount the platform is unwise and unsafe.

Think about it. I can just envision some anointed but nervous preacher running for his life at the site of oncoming preachers rushing the stage. I can also see another problem. Some preachers, deacons and security personnel are packing more than

Bibles these days. If you run up on the wrong one you might get more than a holy hug.

It can be a distraction.

One of the strengths of black worship services is that they are not monolithic. Meaning, some are conservative, some are liberal. Some are traditional, some are contemporary. Some are emotional, some are cerebral.

The same can be said of the people who attend black worship services, including preachers. It's our responsibility to consider not only our own needs but also the needs of those around us. Multiple preachers on the platform can be a physical or mental distraction.

It can misrepresent preaching.

Preaching is not performance art. We should be careful not to signal that it is. It's much deeper than that. Preaching is central to the worship service. And the primary audience in worship is not sitting in front of us but above us. Now don't get it twisted. We should absolutely expect to be engaged and blessed by the sermon and the service. (Ephesians 5:19) But we should be mindful of the dynamics, expectations and responsibilities of the preaching moment.

Now, I recognize that I'm walking on very subjective ground here. One man's "too much" is another man's "too little." What works in one setting, is inappropriate in another. And I'm a strong advocate for walking, waving, weeping, standing and shouting as appropriate worship expressions in the right context. If anything, we have too little Spirit-inspired emotion in our worship services, not too much.

But what I am saying is that there are limits. There are considerations. There are boundaries. Celebration should stop at the floor.

22

WHY FREDDY HAYNES IS SPEAKING AT PELC

So what happened? How did Freddy Haynes get the nod? Nothing controversial here. I could have asked the same question about Debleaire Snell or Roger Bernard or Gina Spivey Brown. I want you to take a quick journey with me.

Rarely a week passes without me receiving a request from some talented man or woman to present at PELC. So, let me give you a peek behind the curtain. Let's look at the process for selecting speakers and presenters at the Pastoral Evangelism and Leadership Council (PELC).

Encounter. Equip. Explode.

Since 1979 PELC, originally Evangelism Council, has brought men and women together from across the globe for leadership training and motivation. It is the largest and longest-running conference of its kind in the denomination. I doubt if E.E. Cleveland, Charles Dudley, Mervyn Warren and the other founders could have envisioned the growth and impact of the conference.

The sermons, plenaries, workshops and boot camps are designed to equip us for effective ministry. We emphasize leadership themes on Mondays and evangelism is our focus on Tuesdays, but we are flexible. Our Wednesday boot camps have doubled in size, and this year the line-up is exceptional.

We want an encounter with God. We want to be equipped for service. We want to explode from Huntsville to make a difference in our communities. Leading God's people is no easy task. So, we pray for and plan worship services that will make dry bones live!

PELC Steering Committee

I'll never forget the first time I was invited to preach at Evangelism Council. I was shaking hands with the late Elder E.E. Cleveland after one of his messages and he said, "Young man, I want you to open up for us this year." That was it. It wasn't a question. It was a command. He was the committee! I loved Dr. Cleveland, but it doesn't work quite like that today.

The PELC steering committee is made up of approximately 30 members. They include the Director of the Office of Regional Conference Ministries and the Ministerial Directors of the N.A.D., Southern Union, and regional conferences. There are west coast representatives, Hispanic caucus representatives, United Kingdom representatives, and a large number of pastoral representatives from across the country. The most effective way to present at PELC is to have a talk with your Ministerial Director or any of the other members. Their names are listed each year in our program.

PELC Theme

Each year before the last pastor has boarded a plane to leave Huntsville, the steering committee has already brainstormed and prayed that the Lord will give us His theme for the following year. In January or February, the committee gathers to spend a few days selecting the theme and planning the conference.

Once the theme has been selected, it influences every decision we make from that point forward. From plenaries to preachers to presenters. The theme is what influences each selection. It's the primary reason that some great presentations or preachers are not included in a particular year. It's not personal. More often than not, it's the theme. The theme for PELC 2017 was **M28: Refocus.**

23

WHAT DO THEY SEE WHEN WE SAY ADVENTIST?

What do people see when they hear Adventist? What words or images come to mind?

For many years I have asked this very question to Adventists and non-Adventists alike in a word association exercise I use in evangelism. The responses have been fairly consistent: Ellen White, Loma Linda, Sabbath, vegetarian, health, and the list goes on. I have asked this questions from Indonesia to Indiana, from Brooklyn to Bermuda. It is interesting to me that of all the responses I've heard over the years, I have never once heard the words, Jesus or love. Not once. It seems that we have a brand problem.

An entire cottage industry has sprung up around the importance of branding. Conferences. Seminars. Webinars. Everyone seems to be pushing the importance of a good brand. And what exactly is a brand? Well, a brand is defined in a number of ways:

- A brand is a concept, service, or product that is publicly distinguished from other concepts, services, or products so that it can be easily communicated and marketed.
- A brand is a feature that distinguishes one product from another.
- A brand is an identifying mark that distinguishes a product.

Similar definitions, but the one I like the most, I found in Forbes magazine. **"Simply put, your brand is what your prospect thinks of when he or she hears your brand name!"** [1]

Exactly. So, let me repeat. The responses to this Adventist word association exercise indicate that we have a brand problem. And the problem with the Adventist brand is not that we are known by the wrong things, but that we are not known by the main thing.

And what is that main thing? What should distinguish us? What should be our brand? Well, Ellen White mentions it in a familiar quote.

"Of all professing Christians, Seventh-day Adventists should be foremost in uplifting Christ before the world." (Gospel Workers p.154)

Now I know that my survey is unscientific and anecdotal. I know that there are a number of ways to express the love of Christ. And I know that other churches and denominations might evoke the same kind of answers. But those churches are not my concern. It seems to me that over the 20 or so years that I've been asking this question, that *somebody* should have mentioned Jesus! So, what do you think? What do *you* see when they say Adventist? Do we even have a problem, and if so, how do we change it?

---

[1] McLaughlin, Jerry. "What is a Brand Anyway?" Forbes Online, December 21, 2011

Culture

&

Social Justice

24

THREE REASONS I PRAY FOR TRUMP

In November of 2014 an article in Charisma News caught my eye. It was entitled, *"5 Ways to Pray for Government Leaders You Don't Agree With."* The writer began with these words. "The substantial majority of readers of this site do not care for Barack Obama's presidency." He was right. His readers were a part of the vast sea of white evangelicals who saw Obama's presidency as an assault on Christian values.

But his article reminded his readers that Christians are not given the option of letting their disagreements with political leaders – no matter how strong – prevent them from praying for them.

I loved it! I loved the article because I love Obama. I love his courage. I love his character. I love his color. I love his cool. I love him because he loves Motown. I love him because he loves the Chicago Bulls. And most of all, I love him because he loves his family.

But now the script has flipped. The tables have turned. The shoe is on the other foot. My guy is gone and with him, much of my optimism for the political future. The rumor of a post-racial society has been dashed. A clown car of political pundits and radio hosts has made a polarized climate even worse. And to top it all, in this time of crisis, a majority of the Christian church in America has proclaimed the president a hero who is making America "great" again. Their response to practically any criticism of Trump is to deny, deflect or defend. Even when the indefensible words have come from the mouth of Trump himself.

Donald Trump is a walking, talking, breathing representation of practically everything I dislike and distrust in a leader. Which leads me to three reasons that I should be praying for Donald Trump:

I *should* be praying for Donald Trump because God said it. 1 Tim. 2:1-3 (You might find this hard to believe, but I'm not always obedient.)

I *should* be praying for Donald Trump because my distaste for him hurts no one but me. Ps.37:8 (I know that. I'm not there yet. Sue me.)

I *should* be praying for Donald Trump because there is a little "Trump" (read sin) in all of us. John 8:7 (Refer to the previous response.)

Now, those are the reasons that I should be praying for Donald Trump. At some point I'll get there, but for now, these are three valid reasons that I do pray for Donald Trump.

I pray for Trump because I love my family.

Paul counseled Timothy to pray for leaders and those in authority so that we can live a quiet and peaceable life. (1 Tim. 2:1-3). I get my greatest motivation to pray for Trump from my wife, children, grandchildren and family. I don't want them to be subjected to the trauma that comes from living in a country that is under siege politically, socially, or economically. I lived through the 60's with its terrible riots, horrible assassinations and social upheaval. And that was mild compared to the harrowing stories I heard from my elders who witnessed and suffered much worse. I don't want that for my family.

And incidentally, God says pray even when it doesn't seem to make sense. It's important to identify the emperor Paul instructed the people of God to pray for. It was Nero. Under Nero, Christians were viciously persecuted. According to the Roman historian Tacitus, Nero murdered his mother and both wives. Donald Trump is a saint compared to him, but God says to pray for him. Pray for him because when you are praying for him, you are literally praying for your own family.

I pray for Trump because I love my country.

Donald Trump has inadvertently elevated Jeremiah Wright from pariah to prophet. It was Wright who warned that America's dark past is not in the past. Just below the surface of many of our polite conversations is a bigotry that we refuse to face. And you can't fix a problem that you don't face. American history is a crazy quilt of pride and prejudice, love and hate.

But America holds a special place in prophetic history (Rev. 13), and in my heart. Anyone who has had the opportunity to travel as I have, can't help but see the blessing of living in America with all of its challenges. I'm not a fan of the neo-conservative distortion of American exceptionalism, but I do see America as a unique place with unique opportunities.

The Jewish exiles that lived in Babylon were instructed to pray for the peace of the city. (Jer. 29:7) That was strange counsel for a captive people. But again, to pray for the city was actually to pray for themselves. Peace is fragile. Our country has not experienced the horror of war in some time and we are in danger of repeating the mistakes of the past.

I remember the stories my elders told of World War II and the Korean War. I can almost feel the Vietnam War. I sat in front of my television as a boy and saw the names of the soldiers killed in action scroll across the screen every night. Every night, a new list of casualties. Our sons and daughters. Our mothers and Fathers. We have painfully short memories. Our prayers should be for the president to steer this country toward peace.

I pray for Trump because God is in control.

Proverbs 21:1 says, *"The king's heart is like a stream of water in the Lord's hands. God steers the stream."*

God sits in heaven and laughs at kings and rulers who think that they are in control. (Psalm 2:4) God not only has the last laugh, he has the last word.

I believe in the sovereignty of God. God is in control. This fight is fixed, and we win. It might be a hard fight, but it's a fixed fight. It might be a long fight, but it's a fixed fight. So as difficult as it is for me right now to accept the leadership of a thin-skinned president, I have accepted the Lordship of an awesome God.

Trump was elected for a term. God is on the throne for eternity.

He said pray… I'll pray.

25

WHAT THE CHURCH LOST WHEN TRUMP WON

It has been the transition that every Trump supporter dreamed of and every Trump detractor feared; A whirlwind of pen strokes, cabinet appointments, and troubling tweets.

The conservatives got the Scalia-clone they wanted. The homeschoolers got the voucher champion they wanted. And "Saturday Night Live" died and went to heaven.

But I'm sad for the church. I love the church. I have devoted my life to the church. To be sure, the church is not monolithic. There are churches of every color and conviction. But these days when you hear "church", most people envision a certain church. It's the "American" church. It's a Protestant church. It's a Bible-believing, evangelical church. It's the church of the media. It's Billy Graham. It's TBN. It's CBN.

This "church" has been joined at the hip to Donald Trump. Over 80% of white evangelicals voted for Donald Trump. I made that point in this tweet that went out shortly after the presidential election, "Trump polling: White evangelicals – 81%. Ku Klux Klan – 100%. Explanation? Possible. Optics? Terrible. Damage? Unbelievable!"

I think that the "church" lost several things on the night that Donald Trump won. Let's take a look at the things that were lost.

The Church lost moral authority.

Let's be clear. There is nothing uglier than Christians throwing stones, but this idea that Christians should prayerfully support and not judge Trump is only partially true. It is not only unwise but it's unbiblical. We are encouraged to judge actions and not motives. (Matthew 7:16; Matthew 12:34) So let's do a little Trump "fruit inspection."

- When columnist Frank Luntz asked Trump if he has ever asked God for forgiveness, Trumps' response was, "I don't think so. I think if I do something wrong, I think, I just try and make it right. I don't bring God into that picture." [1]
- Trump was taped bragging about grabbing women's private parts and accused by a number of women of doing just that.
- Trump's tweets and comments demonstrate his tendency to respond to any and every slight or attack by responding in kind. In other words, if they go low, he goes lower.

Frankly, the problem here is not that Trump made and will continue to make mistakes. We all do! We all will. If we had the glare of the media on our every move, they would possibly find as much if not more. The problem is the church's response to his mistakes. Rather than speaking truth to power, or offering Godly counsel or accountability, the church has tended to deny, downplay, or deflect his comments. The cost is a loss of moral authority.

The Church lost minority support.

I noted earlier that over 80% of white evangelicals voted for Donald Trump. The numbers were the exact opposite among African-Americans. That kind of opposition from people of color in general, (and African-Americans in particular) illustrates more than a blind allegiance to the Democratic Party. It speaks of a deep fear of some of the policies and positions that Trump and the Republican Party hold.

Think about it. Where you stand on policies is driven by where you sit. In other words, your view of policies is driven by how those policies impact your daily life. And people of color are looking at: affordable housing, the criminal justice system, public school funding, gun control, affordable health care, banking and lending policies and a host of other issues from a completely different vantage point than most Anglos.

Personally, I don't think that Trump will be as bad on certain minority issues as some fear. As a professor at an HBCU (Historically Black Colleges and Universities), I'm reminded that some of our best fiscal years were under the Republicans for reasons that are beyond the scope of this article. And I also believe that some Democratic politicians have come painfully close to taking minority support for granted. But on balance, the Trump years look to be challenging years in the minority community–at least in the short term–and that will cost minority support.

The Church lost religious liberty.

I'll probably get push back here because Trump's mouth says that he supports religious liberty. And he has illustrated it by giving priority to Christians who are being persecuted abroad.[2]

But as much as I appreciate the support for persecuted Christians, Trump's actions look less like religious liberty and more like religious patronage. Support for those who have supported him.

And the Muslim ban is just that. It is a ban on individuals based on their religious beliefs. Perhaps Trump could have argued that he did not have that intent, but unfortunately for him, he has a "friend" named Giuliani who gave everyone an inside view and direct quote from Trump who, "asked for a Muslim ban and ordered a commission to do it legally."[3]

I understand that we are dealing with security issues that are nuanced. They defy neat and tidy answers. And I'm certainly not against border security that protects us from dangerous regions and religious fanatics. But when religious affiliation drives the decision of who gets in and who stays out, religious liberty can shift into religious persecution in the blink of an eye. And for those of us who hold religious beliefs that are out of the mainstream, it's just a matter of time before the targeted outsider becomes…us!

I'm done with my Trump commentary for now. This blog was primarily devoted to issues of church leadership, missiology, creative church growth, and trending religious topics. But one of our primary roles as Christian believers is to be the salt of the earth. (Matt. 5) Salt flavors. Salt preserves. And at times, salt…irritates!

1. "Trump Believes in God But Hasn't Asked For Forgiveness" CNN Politics, July 18, 2015. Eugene Scott

2. "Where Christian Leaders Stand On Trumps Refugee Policy" The Atlantic January 27, 2017. Emma Green

3. "Trump asked for a Muslim ban", Giuliani says," and ordered a commission to do it legally." The Washington Post Online, January 29, 2017 Amy B. Wang

26

WHEN SOME TRUMP CRITICISM IS JUST...DUMB

If you're going to speak truth to power, it would help if you'd speak the truth. This was the final blog in my Trump trilogy. Each week this blog addressed church ministry themes: leadership development, research, missiology, trending topics, etc. I didn't mean to do three Trump posts, but every time I tried to stop, "you just kept dragging me back in!" (Gratuitous "Godfather" reference.)

I am no fan of Donald Trump. That's clear for all to see. He's the President. I respect the office. And when I take my own advice, I pray for him. But it'll be a while before I get over this one. This President, in my opinion, dog whistles to this nation's dark side.

For instance, for 5 years, despite the evidence to the contrary, he led the birther parade that questioned Obama's place of birth. It played to the worst nature of this country. Now he's crying crocodile tears over the explosion of racial tensions that he stoked.

No, I'm not a Trump fan, but I'm also not dumb. And that is exactly how I characterize some of the recent criticism I've seen of Donald Trump. The only thing more frustrating than a backfire is friendly fire. That's when you shoot at someone, but you wound yourself instead. I'm seeing a number of Trump foes suffer self-inflicted wounds these days in the media.

For those of you like me, who have serious reservations about our 45th President; let me point out to you three instances when Trump criticism is just dumb.

When it's Personal

I'm not interested in Trump's hair. I'm not interested in Melania's modeling career. I'm not interested in Ivanka's clothing line. And I'm certainly not interested in attacking his son, who had absolutely no part in his father's decision to run for the presidency.

I'm interested in his policies. Period. There's a reason that Michele Obama advised that, "When they go low, we go high." It's not only good moral advice; it's good strategic advice. It doesn't help your arguments against Trump, his appointments, or his policies if folk won't listen to you because of personal attacks. You might feel better, but you are effectively talking to yourself.

When it's Fictional

If you're going to speak truth to power, it would help if you'd speak the truth. Conspiracy theories, exaggerations and outright lies are just as bad coming from the mouths of Trump defenders as Trump detractors.

Why anyone would intentionally quote Trump out of context is beyond me. He's a walking textbook of questionable material. He's a well that never runs dry. He provides free quotes for the asking. So why make stuff up? Why drop a word from a quote that would accurately explain what he's attempting to say? I've seen it and I've heard it, and once again, it does more harm than good.

When it's Suicidal

By suicidal I mean when attacks on Trump are actually hurting you. For instance, I am suspicious of Trumps "law and order" push. His "concern" about minority crime plays to his base and rings hollow to me. And it doesn't' help that he's influenced by criminal justice "experts" like Sheriff David Clarke, Rudy Giuliani and Jeff Sessions.

But believe me, the folk most concerned about inner-city violence are inner-city residents. They don't support indiscriminate stop and frisk practices, but many of these same residents are pleading for more, well-trained officers on their streets. Unfortunately, I've seen some inner-city leaders bristle at the prospect that Trump could be offering money for additional officers on their streets. Why? Because they question his motivation. Really?

February 27-28, 2017 the White House along with Paul Ryan, and others was hosting HBCU (Historically Black Colleges and Universities) presidents. The presidents will discuss their own priorities and Trump's plans to support these institutions that graduate an amazing percentage of black students. Then the firestorm started.

Some are questioning why the presidents of these institutions would attend the meeting. Why provide a photo op and talking points for a President who in many areas stand for positions that they stand against?

Why? Because they deserve the money and the students need to graduate. And frankly, if we're going to start refusing support because of the sin of the source, we'll all be broke, busted and disgusted. You certainly couldn't receive money from me, and I doubt if I could take any from you.

Here's the thing. Call me a pragmatist, but desperate minority communities don't have the luxury of turning down much-needed government resources because of the source. Frankly, we pay taxes like everyone else. That's our money!

So, listen. The house is on fire. Put out the flames first and debate with the firemen later.

How to Keep HBCU Presidents at Home

It was the mother of all photo ops. You couldn't get away from it. Media outlets everywhere pictured presidents of Historically Black Colleges and Universities (HBCUs) gathered in the White House with President Trump. Of course, the surprise guest was Kellyanne Conway, whose mother evidently forgot to tell her it's impolite to put your feet on the furniture…especially in the Oval office…in the presence of black presidents…who'll be hearing about it forever!

The fallout from the meeting was swift and predictable. Donald Trump has been everything that most people in the black community feared. He has tweeted like an unhinged two-year-old. He has given unqualified support to a broken and biased criminal justice system. He has attempted to undermine the free press to his advantage. He has surrounded himself with black leaders who are not accepted by black people. And he has gone from birther accusations to now claiming that Obama tapped his phones.

So, you knew the HBCU presidents were going to be attacked for meeting with him. Many argued that they were legitimizing an illegitimate president, all for the sake of dollars that they probably will never see. I get it—the argument, that is. I don't agree with the argument, but I get it. In fact, I wrote about it in a previous article, but that's for another day. I have a suggestion for you, whether you agreed with the meeting or not.

This is how you can keep HBCU Presidents at home. You can give HBCUs the support they deserve!

And why do they deserve the support? Because they've earned it. The facts speak for themselves:

- HBCUs enroll just 3% of all African-American students, but they graduate 20% of all African-American undergraduates.
- 80% of all African-American judges are HBCU graduates.
- 70% of all African-American dentists are HBCU graduates.
- 50% of all African-American lawyers are HBCU graduates.
- 40% of all African-American engineers are HBCU graduates. [1][2]

And that's not all. A new Gallup study reveals that "black graduates of HBCUs are more likely than black graduates of other institutions to be thriving – strong, consistent, and progressing- in a number of areas in their lives, particularly in their financial and purpose well-being."[3]

HBCUs accomplish all of this with a tuition rate that is 30% less than comparable institutions. HBCUs are enrolling many students that would not be able to attend or afford to attend a college or university, and they are producing an amazing product with limited resources.

HBCUs need the support of African-Americans in general and HBCU alumni in particular. I love the active debate that surrounds the HBCU Presidents' visit to the White House. It demonstrates interest in an important topic. But it costs absolutely nothing to have these discussions and debates. There's another phrase for that. Talk is cheap! What we need are more people, of all colors, who translate passion into tangible support for the institutions these presidents represent. We need to give back.

I am a proud alumnus of an HBCU. In fact, I'm probably a poster child for HBCUs. Most of my family members are HBCU graduates. From Tennessee State, to LeMoyne-Owen, to Meharry, to Oakwood. And now I'm an HBCU professor, and my wife is a development officer for the United Negro College Fund. And there is one painful lesson I've learned of most black institutions. They lack black support.

For example, fewer than 5% of the alumni of my HBCU give to the University.

That's not an alternative fact. That's the absolute truth. Now, at my HBCU we have a growing Alumni Association whose independent fundraising numbers do reach beyond the 5%. So, let's double it to 10% or triple it to 15%. We still have a lot of work to do.

And so yes, it's currently only 5% at my school, but it's probably not much better at your favorite HBCU. I hope that it is, but it's probably not. Alumni might buy a ticket to a Homecoming football game or Frankie Beverly concert. They might give a check during a weekend dedication service or Alumni weekend. But very few alumni support their own institutions in any tangible way.

To be fair, alumni support is shockingly low at most colleges and universities. But that's not my concern. I also clearly understand the challenges that some have had at their alma maters and the student loan debt that they wrestle with. I get that. The fact is everyone can do something. There is no excuse for the lack of financial support we give to HBCUs that do so much, with so little, for so many.

 Love him or hate him, Donald Trump has forced minorities to understand that the cavalry is not coming.

And frankly, our children are too important to waste time hoping for help to come. We must take care of our own business. We must support our own institutions. And if we don't do that, then we won't have to worry about the presidents because there will be no HBCUs for them to lead.

Three Words That Could Cripple The Race Crisis

There is something strange about the Charlottesville incident. It's not as if any of this caught us by surprise. The alt right has been growing. The Klan has been moving from behind the masks and into the mainstream. Donald Trump has never made a mistake that he'd admit. But something about the Charlottesville incident just seems different.

Perhaps it's because it shattered our stereotypes about the face of extreme racism. They were younger, wealthier, and more educated than many realized.

Perhaps it's because the hatred was so aggressive and transparent. So, unwilling to hide.

Certainly, it's because a young life was lost.

To me it feels a bit like Bill Murray in Ground Hog Day. Every day that the alarm clock rings on race in this country, we seem to jump out of the same side of the bed, relive the same old scripts, and fight the same old battles.

I don't pretend to have all the answers. But I am convinced that there are three words that could cripple the race problem. What are the three words?

Christians With Courage

I didn't say cure the race problem, I said cripple it. In other words, there are some problems that defy easy answers and quick fixes. At times, we forget how recent our sordid slave history in America actually is. The Emancipation Proclamation was just 154 years ago, and it took an additional 2 years before Texas got the message and freed the last slaves…and it seems like they've been trying to get them back ever since.

But I'm the eternal optimist and I think Christians can do what no statehouse can ever do. But it will take courage. A particular kind of courage.

Courage to admit you're living in a glass house

The church can ill afford to throw stones about race. The only group that came close to the Klan's support for Trump and his "make America great again" campaign were White evangelical Christians. They supported him at the rate of 81%. Given the racial divide on both sides of the Trump campaign and presidency, the church walked headlong into a racial buzz saw.

As Adventists, we need to clean our own house. We are a remnant with a race problem. We have never addressed racism on an appropriate scale or in the appropriate forum. It's negatively impacting our structure, it's the elephant in the room in Christian education, and it's hindering our mission.

A couple of weeks ago I wrote about E.E. Cleveland and his amazing contributions to the Adventist church. I didn't write about his lifelong struggle with the church to address its unfairness to minorities. Even the meeting he did in Trinidad, which stands today as the first Adventist campaign to baptize 1000, was marred by racism.

It had reminded me that Dr. Cleveland was actually sent to the island as punishment. The brethren switched his assignment from Jamaica to Trinidad, an island that was heavily Catholic. The idea was that he could have no real success there, but God had another idea. He always does. Have things improved? Certainly. But we have a way to go. And God can't fix a problem that we won't face.

Courage to confront the man in the mirror

Peter was a courageous disciple of Christ, but Acts 10 revealed that he had a race problem. That's not surprising. We are all works in progress and dealing with racism is hard work. But it starts with the man in the mirror. What are your feelings about "others?" Better yet, what are your actions toward "others?"

At times, a clearer referendum on your racial attitudes is who you listen to, agree with, and disagree with. When I lived in Southern California, a friend of mine sounded more like Rush Limbaugh than Rush Limbaugh, because that's all he listened to. Whether you are a Limbaugh devotee or not, you must admit that he's an extremely polarizing figure in the area of race. So, what does your fascination with Limbaugh or any other flame thrower say about you and the race issue?

Courage to say something if you see something

The reason the Klan and Neo-Nazis are so comfortable in public is because they are not being challenged in private. What do you say to the racism you hear in private? Nothing throws cold water on a racist joke quicker than dead silence. How many of those tiki-torch bearing young men in Virginia could have been diverted if a courageous Christian friend had confronted them in private.

I cringe at the thought of how many times I've been silent in the face of evil and I'm not alone. Racism has to be confronted and corrected in the context of relationships for it to be effective.

Courage to stop blaming the victim

Perhaps Donald Trump's greatest mistake in speaking to the Virginia tragedy was his "many sides" remark. "There were good and bad people on both sides", he said. It's a false equivalence- describing a situation as if there is a logical equivalence on both sides of an issue, when there is none.

Even if you accept Trump's statement that there was "bad" on both sides, the sheer numbers and degree of evil on the right was far greater. Not to mention the fact that they were "bad" enough to take an innocent girls life. It allows the President to criticize the alt right and avoids alienating some in his base -but it blames the victim.

Racism in the United States has been a blight on the soul and psyche of this nation. It has infected blacks and whites alike- but not to the same degree. By any objective and reasonable measure, the negative impact of racism has been far greater on people of color, particularly black people. Slavery, Jim Crow laws, redlining in housing, discrimination in college admission, and a list of other evils have unequally impacted black people.

And the negative impact of racism continues to this day. Recently the Corporation for Enterprise Development released a study that showed it would take black families 228 years to amass the same amount of wealth that white families have today. The argument that racism is an equal opportunity offender is a lie that stalls honest discussion.

Even in the church there are those who never miss an opportunity to remind black people that they must deal with racism in their own ranks. I accept that. But if you lead with that, or if you don't accept the reality that one side has been damaged more and is in greater need of resources, the discussion is dishonest.

Courage to vote

I didn't plan to, but I'll throw this in.

I woke up this morning to Donald Trump twitter bombing his critics and doubling down on his earlier statements about the Virginia tragedy. Now he's arguing that the," culture of our great country is being ripped apart by the removal of our beautiful statues and monuments." Confederate monuments. Whether you agree with him or not, you must agree that statements like these and others are terrible for race relations.

Listen, I believe in the sovereignty of God. He has worked out his will in seasons far worse than this. The tweets of Trump are nothing like the madness of Nero and others and we're instructed to pray for them all. But you don't just get the government you pray for; you get the government you vote for.

I'm done.

29

WHY ADVENTIST MINISTERS MARCH

It was 6 a.m. Monday morning. I was dog tired, but on a plane to Washington D.C. For a moment, I wondered if I'd made a smart decision. Classes just started, and I was also conducting a 2-week revival. I only had time to fly in and fly out. But it turned out to be a day that I won't soon forget.

Al Sharpton and the National Action Network had invited 1000 ministers to celebrate the 54th anniversary of Dr. Martin King's March on Washington. They wanted to bring attention to a number of issues, including:

- A nation still struggling with issues of race and class.
- The racist "tiki- torch" march in Charlottesville and the murder of Heather Heyer.
- The growing problem of voter suppression.
- The plague of mass incarceration and a broken criminal justice system.

The plan was for 1000 Ministers to march from the King monument to the steps of the Department of Justice, with a rally to follow. The number of registered ministers had grown to over 3000 well before the march even began. The sight was amazing. There were ministers from numerous faith traditions. Some in robes, some in collars, some in suits, some came casual. There seemed to be almost as many Anglo ministers as ministers of color. And the number of Adventist ministers was obvious and impressive.

That's right. The Adventist ministers were out in force. Ironic, because the Adventist community has a well-earned reputation for avoiding social justice issues. A younger generation has brought a different sensibility and things are changing. But let me give you a few reasons that Adventist ministers have marched in the past and continue to march today.

Because We Missed Too Many Marches

In the spring of 1999, I was the director of a steering committee addressing police misconduct in Southern California. I was asked to participate in a press conference conducted by CNN. When the moderator identified me as a Seventh Day Adventist, the CNN reporter said something I'll never forget. He said, "The Adventists are involved? *Everybody* must be on board!!" That was not a compliment.

There are dangers when justice is your passion. The actors and issues and camps change at lightning speed. Sometimes you can find yourself on the wrong side of certain ethical issues. But the danger of being written off by the community as selfish and unconcerned is just as bad, if not worse. We were largely on the sidelines of the civil rights movement and our reputation will never fully recover. We can't make that mistake again.

Because We Honor Those Who Did March

I am excited about a new generation of social justice activists in the Adventist church. But it's clear that many of them don't know their history. At a time when the church was as racist as the crowd that King marched against, we had a "remnant" that spoke truth to power inside and outside the church. The names Frank Hale, Randy Stafford, Earl Moore, Jacob Justice, J. Paul

Monk, Warren Banfield, Mylas Martin, and Charles Joseph are a few that come to mind.

Because Marching Can Still Make a Difference

Charlottesville proved that. It's hard to get the images out of your head. Marches can still make a powerful statement-positively and negatively. They are smaller and less meaningful today than in times past, but that's understandable. The issues have changed. When you are marching for concerns that affect you personally and painfully, like desegregating schools and ending the Vietnam War, then you can expect larger, more passionate crowds.

Marches aren't the only way to make an important statement, and in many cases, not even the best way. I think local activism; voter registration drives and targeted economic boycotts are more effective. But when they are carefully connected to future plans, marches can still be the catalyst for lasting change.

Because Jesus was at the March

How do I know? Because the theme lined up with His mission. In Luke 4 and Matthew 25, Jesus made his priorities clear. He came to heal spiritually and physically. Follow Jesus and you find him:

- Defending the oppressed
- Feeding the hungry
- Standing for women's rights in a sexist culture
- Identifying with those behind prison walls
- Speaking for widows, orphans, and immigrants...I mean strangers

I repeat. There are real dangers for ministers and churches involved in social justice issues. Your witness can be weakened when people lump you into a particular party or movement. Your time can be consumed by never ending problems. It's not for the faint of heart. But Christ's simple charge to us is, as the father has sent me into the world, so send I You. (John 17:18)

My plane hadn't landed at home before the predictable criticism began.

"That's not what Adventist ministers do."

"Why are you involved in secular fights? Let God take care of it."

"It's just a lot of race baiting."

"Let's not get involved in politics."

I appreciate the counsel. That's the beauty of America. We can agree, disagree, or agree to disagree. I support your right to criticize marchers. In fact, if anyone ever tries to take away your right to criticize marchers...we'll march against that!

30

THE SHARPTON I KNOW

As soon as I saw the flyer I knew there would be a fight. *"Special Worship Experience with Carlton Byrd. Special Guest-Al Sharpton."* It was a much-needed community rally sponsored by the Oakwood University church. Dr. Byrd began the assembly with an address on unity in diversity and Sharpton followed.

By most accounts Sharpton's message, that ranged from voting rights to immigration policy, was thoughtful and well received. But I was right. The critics were out in force. Online and in person they blasted the church and Sharpton before, during, and after the presentation.

Sharpton is the founder and director of the National Action Network. Founded in 1991, it is a major civil rights organization with chapters throughout America. From his earliest days as an activist in New York, Sharpton has always been a polarizing figure. Sharpton's supporters hail him as a champion for the oppressed. Sharpton's detractors blame him for deteriorating race relations in America.

But issues like police misconduct, civil rights, and civil rights leaders look different depending on who you are and where you are. As Nelson Mandela was fond of saying, *"Where you stand depends on where you sit."* And in early 1999, Al Sharpton and I were sitting in a Marriott hotel in Riverside, California discussing ways to calm a community that was about to explode.

On December 28, 1998, a young lady by the name of Tyisha Miller was driving her aunt's car in Riverside, California and her tire went flat. As she waited for help in her locked car, she had a seizure. Officers were alerted, came to the locked car, and found her foaming at the mouth and shaking. She had a gun in her car for protection and the officers claimed that she reached for it when she came out of her coma. They opened fire 23 times. 12 of the bullets hit Miller- 4 in the head.

The city exploded. Long standing tensions between the minority community and law enforcement resurfaced. I was asked by the family and religious community to lead a steering community to address the volatile issue. Months of press conferences, marches, and court cases followed. The full story is for another day, but it brings me back to the hotel room with Sharpton.

Over a two-year, period, I came to know civil rights leaders from Martin King III to Jesse Jackson to Dick Gregory to the late Johnny Cochran. Each of them was helpful, but none of them made the difference that Sharpton did. These are some of the things I came to know about him.

He'll come when you call him

Many of the critics of Sharpton, Jesse Jackson, and others accuse them of being ambulance chasers and publicity hounds. The accusation is that they troll for racial and social problems and then make them worse when they show up. The reality is that most of the time both Jackson and Sharpton are invited by the immediate family to come and help.

As tragic as Tyisha Miller's death was, it remained a fairly local issue until the family got Sharpton and his crowd involved. When he came the national media came with him and issues of police misconduct in Riverside became national news. He was hard working and very sensitive to the needs of the family. And none of his efforts cost the family or the steering committee a dime.

He might get you arrested

Even before Sharpton hit the ground in Riverside, there was talk of civil disobedience - going to jail as a form of protest. People had been marching by the thousands but the police officers who shot Tyisha Miller had still not been fired or even disciplined. The community was getting restless and dangerous. Sharpton suggested that we conduct a major march to the downtown police headquarters, block the entrance, and force our arrest. The publicity would force the city to move.

Well, I quickly found out that the clergy in Riverside was not as eager as the clergy in Birmingham and Montgomery to go to jail. Some of them reminded me that this wasn't the 60s. Some of them reminded me that they had unpaid traffic tickets! But there I was, leading from the front. In charge and eventually in jail.

He's not always consistent

It could have been my ears, but I thought I heard Sharpton and Dick Gregory say, "Don't worry brothers and sisters. We'll be the first ones in and the last ones out! We'll be the first ones arrested and the last ones released!" That was particularly encouraging to a reluctant band of leaders, some of whom weren't sure if they could get out of jail as easily as they could get in.

True to his word, Sharpton was the first to be arrested. I was in the next wave, about 15 minutes behind. As I walked into the holding area with my friend Robert Edwards, who did I see walking out of the holding area but Al Sharpton and Dick Gregory. It's probably not appropriate to reveal what I thought or said, but so much for the first being last and the last being first! He's human.

He was always courageous

The quality I respected most in Sharpton was his courage. He was absolutely fearless. Under constant attack from law enforcement. Misquoted by the media. Second guessed by even some of the victims he attempted to help. He never wavered. He came early, worked hard, and stayed late. You don't really understand or appreciate the Sharpton's of the world until you need their help.

Sharpton and I disagree on some significant subjects. But we need more people willing to publicly stand for what they believe. People with the courage to speak for those who can't effectively speak for themselves. Because at some point, you might very well need someone to advocate for you. Martin Niemoller, a pastor who spent years in a Nazi concentration camp put it this way.

> First, they came for the Socialists, and I did not speak out --
> Because I was not a Socialist.
>
> Then they came for the Trade Unionists, and I did not speak out -
> Because I was not a Trade Unionist.
>
> Then they came for the Jews, and I did not speak out—
> Because I was not a Jew.
>
> Then they came for me—and there was no one left to speak *for me*.

31

MICHAEL NIXON, ANDREWS U, AND RACE

Historically, I've never been a big Andrews University fan. I graduated from Andrews, but in the same way you graduate from reform school or drivers school – I had to go. I was fresh out of Oakwood, and newly sponsored to pursue my call to ministry. The last thing that I wanted to see was snow in early October. But there I was in Michigan, teeth chattering, body shivering, and wondering why my ears wouldn't stop itching. Welcome to frostbite. Welcome to Andrews.

In short order Andrews reaffirmed many of my past perceptions of conservative Anglos in general and Adventist Anglos in particular. It was a place where, despite the diversity, white was "normal" and everything else was "ethnic." I'm convinced that if they had asked the campus community to paint a picture of Jesus, the prevailing portrait would have been a blue eyed, English speaking, white man.... who loved 3 ABN.

So, in light of all that, what has happened on Andrew's campus since February is nothing short of an act of God to me. As you can see, I'm not shy about sharing my view of Andrew's stumbles, so I'll be equally as willing to share my kudos.

You probably know the story by now.

On February 9-11, 2017 Pastor Jaime Kowlessar lit a fire under the campus when he spoke for Black History Weekend. He was accused by some of partisan, divisive speech. He touched on issues of social justice and the impact of a Trump presidency.

His messages caused such a stir on campus and in the community, that the University issued an apology. Bad idea. That apology from the University insulted and enflamed many Black students on campus.

On Feb. 18, Chaplain Mike Polite and other students released the, "It's Time AU", video. The video demanded an apology from the University for systemic racism and called for plans to address the long- standing problem.

On February 23, President Andrea Luxton addressed the volatile issue at a University chapel service. The video she showed and remarks she made shook the University and stirred the church.

Before I continue with the story let me note this. The leadership that President Dr. Luxton provided is not just proof of unusual gifts but it underscores our desperate need for female leadership at every level of the Adventist church. My hunch is that Andrews would still be searching for a solution if a gentleman had been at the helm. We're attempting to provide leadership in a complex world with one hand- a female hand- tied behind our backs. But that's for another day.

I want to look at three powerful things that have taken place on that campus since that racial explosion. Three positive developments that I didn't see coming. Three things that are a lesson to anyone interested in genuine racial reconciliation.

The Apology

The apology that Dr. Luxton extended to the protestors and the Andrews community was a study in effective reconciliation. Two things stood out to me.

It was swift – Dr. Luxton's response was quick. Even before she spoke to the campus community on February 23 at the University chapel, she had already sent out an email apologizing for Andrew's racism. The "It's Time AU" demand for a swift response certainly aided this, but you get the sense that the president didn't need to be prodded. She moved, and she moved fast.

It was sincere. Now, it's impossible to read a person's heart, but you can read their words and later review their actions. This is what Dr. Luxton said:

"We have not listened well…"

"We have not been sensitive and taken action when action should have been taken."

"We never have an excuse to devalue, or make assumptions of another because of their race."

"We are profoundly sorry!"

There it is. None of this, "if I've hurt you," or "if you think I've done anything wrong" language. She was clear about the problem and direct in her apology. No hedging. No dodging. No excuses. That's an apology.

The Action Plans

At the University chapel, Dr. Luxton continued to address the problem of historical and systemic racism by listing important steps to correct the problem. In brief:

- Diversity training for each group on campus; faculty, staff, and students.
- A priority on diversity in hiring with regular progress reports.
- A strengthened grievance process for reporting and resolving injustice and mistreatment.
- A commitment to honor, celebrate, and support different worship expressions.

An immediate search for a full-time, senior level administrator of diversity who reports directly to the President.

Now, here is where most great ideas and reformations stall. It's a lot easier to talk about change than it is to execute change. The road from vision to action is littered with casualties. Talk is cheap. So, it was here that I was most skeptical, but it was here that I was most surprised and most gratified.

The Appointment

On July 6, 2016, President Luxton announced the University's first Vice President for Diversity and Inclusion, Attorney Michael Timothy Nixon. He began his duties on August 1. It's not often that organizations hit a home run, but this is nothing short of that.

Nixon wasn't a safe pick. Raised in Berrien Springs and a graduate of Andrews Academy, he has experienced first- hand the challenges of racial ignorance and insensitivity in that college town. He tells of the fall-out at Andrews Academy from a presentation his father did on race and the Bible. But in reality, he's a perfect choice.

- He is under 30 and has the sensibility of a generation the church sorely needs.
- He is uniquely prepared as an attorney and former legal coordinator for the Fair Housing Justice Center in New York City. He founded the Office of Service and Social Action at the University of Saint Francis.
- He has the confidence of the community. He has for years been one of them.
- He is the product of amazing parents, Dr. Timothy and Dr. Sandria Nixon. His ability to support and challenge the university at the same time is a direct reflection of his parents.
- He loves the gospel, he loves people and he has a great sense of humor-and he'll need it!
- He has the courage to speak truth to power.

When I see Michael Nixon, I'm hopeful for the future of race relations at Andrews and the church. Over the course of his work at Andrews, I'm sure we'll disagree on certain ideas and approaches. I reflect my generations skepticism- read cynicism- of the prospect of meaningful racial reconciliation. But he listens well, and his judgment is sound.

Andrews University is still not one of my destination spots. Location alone will always work against that. But my respect for the institution has grown immensely. They have demonstrated amazing vision, decisive action, and Christian courage in the wake of a race crisis. Good example. Great job.

LEADERSHIP ICONS

32

MINISTERS WHO MARKED MY MINISTRY-
BISHOP GILBERT PATTERSON

Memphis, Tennessee is a city of churches. Always has been and always will be. At one time, it was listed as the city with more churches per capita than any city in America. Churches large and small dot the landscape of my hometown, but the denomination that is perhaps the king of the hill in Memphis is the Church of God in Christ whose international headquarters are based in the city.

The Church of God in Christ (COGIC) is the largest Pentecostal denomination in the world with more than 6 million members worldwide. On November 14, 2000, the city of Memphis was excited because Bishop Gilbert Patterson, for years one of the most creative religious forces in the city, was elected Presiding Bishop, the top position of leadership in the church. The world was about to see what we'd seen for years. Bishop Patterson was a unique gift to the body of Christ that doesn't come around very often.

In the late 70s, I was home for the weekend from Oakwood College and we decided to catch a Friday night service at Temple of Deliverance church. It was the fastest growing church in the city at that time and Bishop Patterson was the pastor. I had attended the church on a number of occasions, mainly for concerts and choir rehearsals, but I'd never met Bishop Patterson. So, it came as a complete surprise to me as we walked into the balcony of the church to hear his words directed at me from the desk, "Good to see you Reverend."

No formal introduction, but he obviously knew more about me than I was aware. Ironic, because I never had the opportunity to explain to Bishop Patterson how his ministry influenced mine. Let me share it with you. These are some Patterson characteristics that influenced me.

He had a heart for social justice

In 1968, Dr. Martin King came to Memphis to support the sanitation workers strike. It became the setting for his assassination on April 4 of that year. Bishop Patterson was a major player in that strike that changed the city and tragically impacted the world. He was never a very visible or vocal front line civil rights figure in Memphis, but he was always strategically and financially involved.

He was an amazing administrator

Bishop Patterson began his ministry in his teens. He became the co-pastor of the Holy Temple COGIC with his father W.A. Patterson in 1962. He left that little church in 1975 to establish the Temple of Deliverance near downtown Memphis. The membership grew to 15,000 people with an active membership approaching 7,000.

He seemed to be able to juggle a number of prominent projects at the same time; day care, Podium Records, WBBP radio station, academy, radio broadcast, and television ministry. In 1978, the congregation opened its new sanctuary to accommodate the explosive growth. At the time Jet Magazine noted that it was the first million-dollar church built by African Americans in Memphis.

He was a gifted preacher

Before he passed in 2007, Bishop Patterson was one of the most sought-after speakers in the country. He turned the stereotype of the uneducated, unprepared Pentecostal preacher on its head. His specialty was unpacking the narratives of the Old Testament. And for those who don't appreciate the African American folk art and spiritual passion of "whooping", they've never really listened to Bishop Patterson.

He was a strategic church programmer

In 1996, the book *Natural Church Development by Christian Schwarz* was released. It became an international manual for growing healthy churches. It identified characteristics and growth factors that most healthy, growing churches possess.

Two of the growth factors are energy transformation and interdependence. The idea is that church ministries and programs are not islands. They function best when the energy and resources of one program seamlessly lift up other programs. Some pastors have a gift for creating a church calendar that is not just busy but creates a tide that takes other ministries up with it. Dr. Carlton Byrd is an example at the Oakwood University church. Bishop Patterson was a master.

The church calendar was carefully choreographed to generate movement and momentum. It kept the staff and volunteers busy, but it created an atmosphere that attracted visitors and kept members connected, excited, and involved.

Those are just a few of the characteristics of Bishop Patterson that marked my ministry. We never really know the impact our lives have on others.

33

MINISTERS WHO MARKED MY MINISTRY: PASTOR ROBERT LESLIE WILLIS

I have spent the last several years of my life developing religious leaders, particularly pastors. I have researched and interviewed the best and the brightest. But I'm convinced that if you look up the word "pastor" in the dictionary, you'll probably see a picture of R.L. Willis looking back at you. Or at least you should. He was about as good as it gets.

I'm not talking about what I heard, I'm telling you what I saw. He pastored my home church in Memphis, Tennessee during the turbulent 70s and no one has had a greater impact on my ministry. And the same could be said by a great number of pastors.

Born in Brooklyn, New York 87 years ago, he passed away in November of 2012. Elder Willis pastored some of the most significant churches in the North American division. He was a man of extraordinary gifts and compassion and these are some of the things about his ministry that stood out.

He had a passion for pastoring

Elder Willis was singularly gifted in a number of different areas. He was an evangelist, a builder, a printer, a stewardship expert, a careful administrator, and the list goes on. But his unmistakable passion was pastoring the local church.

He was always in demand and received numerous invitations to serve on various levels of the denomination. In fact, he actually accepted an offer from the Southern Union to serve in the Ministerial Department. But it was only two years before the call of the local church was too much, and he returned to his first love.

This is an age of ministry specialization. Young men and women have opportunities to be more specific about how and where they would like to serve the church. At times, it seems as if pastoral ministry is just a temporary stop for some who have other stops in mind. It's refreshing to observe leaders who pastor, not because they have to, but because they want to.

He was an advocate for young people

Elder Willis knew the value of pastoring across the generational divide, but it was clear that he had a real heart for young people. He encouraged our ideas, ignored our arrogance, tolerated our music, participated in our activities and always pushed, pushed, pushed us to our potential.

As young people, we were involved in the life of the church. I remember when he told me I was going to preach my first sermon. He provided the books and counsel. He probably regretted it when I preached, "The Games People Play" and tried to whip everything and everybody in the church! But as usual he was there to suggest and support.

He was a mentor of ministers

The number of young men Elder Willis inspired to enter the pastoral ministry is amazing! I won't go into names, but it reads like a who's who in Adventist ministry. It is a testament to the impact he had on the lives and the call of young men.

And it was not that his ministry gave some sanitized, sugar-coated view of the local church. He had serious battles in the local church. At times, I thought he was going to literally come to blows with some of the "saints" who pushed the wrong button. But he was real and that made his ministry real.

He was a church growth pioneer

Most of what I learned about effective church growth and evangelism I observed in Elder Willis. He was one of the most productive pastoral evangelists I have ever witnessed. His public meetings were well planned and organized. He regularly baptized over 100 souls in a calendar year. But that was because his public meetings were just the highlight of his year-round evangelistic program.

Every Sabbath souls responded to his Christ centered messages, holistic worship services, and powerful appeals. We were literally growing all year long.

He prioritized prayer

I'll never forget the advice he gave me to prepare my public prayers as carefully as I prepared my sermons. I remember the sermons on prayer, the books on prayer, the mid-week prayer meetings, and the all-night prayer sessions. It gave me a sense of the importance of prayer that influences me to this day.

He was a family man

Blessed with four talented daughters and a beautiful wife, Elder Willis pastored in an age when many first families seemed second to the church. But it was clear to all that as much as Elder Willis loved his church and his ministry, they were a distant second to his family.

He preached the cross

Of all the things that singled him out, nothing set Willis apart like the way he preached the cross. Each of us who sat at his feet have vivid memories of the weekly appeals that inevitably landed at Calvary. He painted a picture so vivid of the Master's sacrifice that it was impossible not to be moved.

Ours was an age of deep legalism. There were all kinds of off-shoots working inside and outside the church. But the Christ centered preaching of Elder Willis allowed many of us to escape relatively unscathed. He was a master of balance in a church that often leaned too far to the right.

I could go on. I've only scratched the surface on the amazing impact of Pastor Robert Leslie Willis. I can't wait to tell him thanks.

Ministers Who Marked My Ministry: Dr. E. E. Cleveland

He was no more than 6'3, but to the world he seemed larger than life. Dr. E. E. Cleveland. I actually heard him before I saw him. As a child, we'd listen to the recording of his 1966 evangelistic campaign in Port of Spain, Trinidad. At the close of that meeting over 1000 people were baptized – a first for the Seventh Day Adventist Church.

Born in Huntsville Alabama in 1921, he was a man of amazing gifts and scholarship. He authored 15 books, lectured regularly at prominent universities, trained over 1000 ministers, and served the church effectively at several levels. He was the most prolific evangelist in the SDA church, baptizing over 16,000 people.

He had a passion for people-especially people of color. He organized a campus chapter of the N.A.A.C.P. at Oakwood College when he was a student. He participated in the historic March on Washington in 1963. He crossed paths with Dr. Martin King and Dr. Ralph Abernathy during the civil rights movement and he was clearly the equivalent of Dr. King to the Adventist Church. He was the co-founder of the Human Relations Committee for the General Conference of SDAs. He was a tireless champion for social justice inside and outside the church.

But the personal encounters and connections are what marked me. Four of them influence me to this day.

Encounter Number One

Dr. Cleveland left the General Conference and came to Oakwood University in 1977. His class on Public Evangelism was probably the most popular class on campus. Attended by religion majors and non-religion majors alike, it was literally standing room only in the classroom. The class was already full when I registered in 1979, but they told me to just go to class and perhaps someone might drop out.

I could hardly get in the door for the press. Somehow, I was able to enroll in the class and every day was amazing! It was part revival, part evangelistic campaign, part college class. The stories, the testimonies, the humor, the passion, the insight. I had never had a classroom experience like that and I've been trying unsuccessfully to reproduce it in my own classroom ever since.

Encounter Number Two

As a religion student, I got to know Dr. Cleveland well. Frankly, I was in awe of him. I would soak in every suggestion and hang on every word. In the late 70s the campus and church community were always struggling with some legalistic teaching or off-shoot group- Shepard's Rods, Brinsmeads, you name it. I set up an appointment to speak to Dr. Cleveland about salvation and sanctification.

He spoke about grace in a way that I'd never heard it before. Tears rolled down his face as he told me:

"We are justified, before we are qualified."

"We are accepted, before we are acceptable."

"We are trusted, before we are trust worthy."

"We are declared perfect, while we are being perfected."

This from a man who preached passionately against sin and who many felt was amazingly arrogant. They didn't quite get him. As powerful a figure as he was, he was sensitive, almost overly so. What I saw was a man who was so grateful for what God had done, that he had no filter sharing it. He was so confident in his salvation, that at times it could be mistaken for overconfidence in himself... and he could be a bit arrogant.

Encounter Number Three

When Dr. Cleveland retired from Oakwood, I was the Director of Church Growth and Discipleship in the Southeastern California conference. For a couple of years, they split his courses across the faculty, but in 2007 they asked me to join the Religion faculty of Oakwood University. My concentration is Church Growth and Evangelism, so I was effectively Dr. Cleveland's successor. I taught his classes.

That year, I accepted the position after the class schedules were printed. Dr. Cleveland's name was still on the class schedule when the students came back from summer break. In short, the students came to class expecting to see E.E. but instead they saw me! It took a minute or two for the students to realize the cruel switch, but when they did...it was NOT pretty!!

I knew how they felt. There was no way anyone could fill Dr. Cleveland's shoes. Certainly not me. But he was always there for encouragement and counsel. I spent hours listening to him. Even as his steps slowed, his mind remained sharp and he was a blessing until the time of his death in August of 2009.

Today

In 2017, I became the Director of the Bradford, Cleveland, Brooks, Leadership Center on the campus of Oakwood University. Our lives intersect again. Today, we are teaching a changing church the unchanging principles that marked these men's ministries. There will never be another E. E. Cleveland, but his contributions live on. I'll make sure of that.

35

THE SECOND THING THAT EVERY LEADER SHOULD DO

I was preaching in Philadelphia not long ago for young pastor Marquis Johns. I had a fantastic time at the North Philly Church. The worship was rich, the fellowship was great, and the church was alive. I sat in the study before and after I preached, observing the endless parade of members into and out of the office. I listened to the buzz of activity that's always present in a growing church. It reminded me how rewarding leading a local church can be.

But it also reminded me of the challenges. Marquis has a clear vision for where he wants the church to go and every gift to get them there. I reminded the church in my remarks that he's a race horse. He reminds me of myself early in my ministry. Surrounded by people. Always pushing. Never satisfied. Self-motivated. Not always listening. He's always going to be at, or near the top of the productivity scale. But at times the personal and professional price is going to be high. I can see it because I've seen it.

But we desperately need Marquis and others like him in these complex times. Why? Because he's a leader. He's creating while others are criticizing. He's a gifted, impatient, stubborn, productive leader. He's going to drive some members crazy, but he's going to get some amazing things done. He's going to make some big mistakes but he's going to make an even bigger mark.

Why did I start this blog with Marquis? Because when I was with him, I was convinced that I needed to complete a blog I released months ago. The blog was entitled, *"The First Thing That Every Leader Should Do!"* And what is that first thing? The first thing that every leader should do is listen. At some point in our time together, I counseled the young preacher to slow down a bit and listen. I was actually recalling some principles I laid out in the earlier blog. The first thing that every leader should do is listen, because:

You Don't Know Everything

No matter how gifted you are, there are gaps in your ability to lead that others can fill. You have to listen and learn before you leap.

You Don't Know Everyone

It's about relationships. Kenneth Blanchard says, "The key to successful leadership today is influence, not authority." You may have arrived at the local church with gifts and a title, but real leadership authority is forged through relationship building.

You Don't Know the Culture

All churches are different. Boundless energy and amazing gifts can bring immediate success, but that success is temporary if it's cut and pasted onto a reluctant culture. Lasting change comes through cultural change. Cultural change calls for listening and learning before you launch out.

But as I was counseling the young "race horse" it was clear to me that my counsel to him was incomplete- and so was my earlier blog. It was good counsel, but it was partial counsel. Because as important as listening is, it's only the first thing that every leader should do. After you have demonstrated the wisdom to listen, you need to muster the courage to lead. The second thing that every leader must do is lead!

And that's what Marquis and other talented leaders are doing. They are leading. It might not be perfect leadership but it's productive leadership. And frankly, there is no such thing as perfect leadership. There will be those on the sidelines who complain, and at times those complaints will be necessary and absolutely accurate. But a good leader can listen and move at the same time. Most of our pressing problems, especially in the church, are actually leadership problems.

We Need Spiritual Leadership

This is the leaders highest call. You can be effective in the board room, or the back room, but if you're a stranger to the prayer room, you're not an effective leader. Church leadership is essentially spiritual leadership.

I have seen a number of surveys that identified the quality people desired most in a leader. The number one quality is almost always integrity. The skills that people value most are soft skills- a combination of social skills and character traits. If a pastor is not pursuing a closer walk with God, eventually it will undermine everything else he does.

We Need Structural Leadership

Spiritual leadership alone is not enough. At some point leaders must come out of their prayer closets and deal with the nuts and bolts of leading difficult change in institutions and people. Andy Stanley reminds us that some problems at church are spiritual, but many are structural. And you can't solve a structural problem by praying about it. In fact, at times prayer can become a convenient excuse or delay.

I was assigned to a church years ago that complained about prayer meeting attendance. The problem, they felt, was that people were not as committed, not as spiritual as they once were. But when I explored the problem I realized that they had scheduled prayer meeting at a time when most of the members were still driving home from work. We changed the time and the attendance spiked. It wasn't a spiritual problem it was a structural problem. Real leaders know the difference.

We Need Strong Leadership

Leadership is not for the faint at heart. You must be strong. The criticism is constant. The rewards are few. Everyone has an opinion. Everyone knows a better way. Everyone has seen it done better somewhere else. But few are prepared to participate or sacrifice.

Now let me be clear. We need leaders who are strong, not leaders who are bullies. We need leaders not bosses. Unfortunately, that's a concept that many leaders don't get.

1 Peter 5:3, warns against "lording" leadership. Leadership that's controlling, independent, and deaf. The tragic fate of a lording leader is that at some point he will need someone to save him from himself, and he will have driven most independent voices away.

So, hats off to the leaders who are not only listening well, but leading well. John Maxwell said that good leaders, "know the way, show the way, and go the way." I like that.

Connect with Author

Dr. Jesse L. Wilson

 www.drjessewilson.com

 drjessewilson@gmail.com

   @drjessewilson

CPSIA information can be obtained
at www.ICGtesting.com
Printed in the USA
FFOW04n0148261117
43753943-42643FF